Praise for The Path of Alchemy

"Mark Stavish has been a prolific writer on alchemy over the years, and this book represents his finest work yet. It is a must for any study of alchemy in understanding the subtle side of its process. He writes with a knowledge and insight that comes from years of experience, and yet the book is presented in an easy-to-read format. Mark's work is quite unique and is a valuable addition to the various alchemical paradigms that are starting to expand through the literary fields."

—Pat Zalewski,
author of *Golden Dawn Enochian Magick*
and *The Kabbalah of the Golden Dawn*

"*The Path of Alchemy* is an insightful, highly practical work, dedicated to the perpetuation of this ancient art and science. It promises what alchemy promises: 'No Work, no result,' as is most certainly the case. Having myself completed all seven years of classes at the Paracelsus Research Society under Frater Albertus himself, I highly recommend this book. Its balance between theory and practice is what the sincere seeker into these Mysteries needs in order to learn from within and accomplish in the 'without.' It is the finest piece of writing—clear, detailed, eclectically sound, and as complete as any work in this area can be—that I have seen in the past three decades. It is as indispensable as is Frater Albertus's own timeless classic, *The Alchemist's Handbook*."

—Joseph C. Lisiewski, Ph.D.,
author of *Ceremonial Magic, Kabbalistic Cycles & the Mastery of Life*,
and *Kabbalistic Handbook for the Practicing Magician*

ABOUT THE AUTHOR

Mark Stavish has published nearly a hundred articles, book reviews, and interviews on the traditions of Western esotericism. He has also served as a consultant to print and broadcast media and several documentaries. In 1998, Stavish founded what became the Institute for Hermetic Studies. In 2001, he established the Louis Claude de St. Martin Fund, a nonprofit fund dedicated to advancing the study and practice of Western esotericism.

pathways to enlightenment

The Path of

Alchemy

ENERGETIC HEALING AND THE
WORLD OF NATURAL MAGIC

Mark Stavish

Llewellyn Publications
Woodbury, Minnesota

First Edition
Seventh Printing, 2014

Book design and layout by Joanna Willis
Cover design by Kevin R. Brown
Cover painting "Alchemist Laboratory," 1570, Jan van der Straet (1523–1605/
    Flemish) © SuperStock, Inc. / SuperStock
Interior illustrations by Llewellyn art department

The publisher and author gratefully acknowledge the Societas Rosicruciana in America Inc. for permission to reprint the excerpt from Francis Mayer's *Mercury* article "The Ancient and Modern Elixirs of the Alchemists."

Llewellyn is a registered trademark of Llewellyn Worldwide Ltd.

Cataloging-in-Publication Data for this title is on file with the Library of Congress.
ISBN 13: 978-0-7387-0903-1
ISBN 10: 0-7387-0903-4

Llewellyn Publications
A Division of Llewellyn Worldwide Ltd.
2143 Wooddale Drive
Woodbury, MN 55125-2989
www.llewellyn.com

Printed in the United States of America

The Path of Alchemy is the compilation of millennia of human striving toward the Light. May it serve as a stepping stone for another generation of seekers, that the chain of the Hermetic tradition continue unbroken for another two thousand years. This book is dedicated to all those who serve the Light and are committed to completing the Great Work.

NOTICE

Use caution and common sense while carrying out the instructions and recipes found in this book. Herbal products must be prepared and used with care.

Many people are allergic to certain plants. Always make sure that the plants you are working with are safe to ingest and that you will not have any allergic reactions to working with them.

Check with a licensed health care professional before ingesting any herbal product. This book is no substitute for proper medical care; consult a doctor for any serious health problems.

You are responsible for your health. The publisher assumes no responsibility for injuries occurring as a result of following the instructions in this book, nor for the efficacy of the recipes.

CONTENTS

FOREWORD

My early steps on the alchemical path occurred when I was less than ten years of age. That would have been, at the latest, 1962—the year that a German alchemist, Albert Riedel, opened a now-legendary school in Utah, the Paracelsus Research Society. In 1984, I entered the beginners' class of his school, to take further steps on this path, and was initiated into the oral tradition of alchemy by Frater Albertus.

I was led to his school by the book *Praxis Spagyrica Philosophica*.[1] It was the first—of perhaps a hundred books concerning alchemy I had searched—to show that the author had personal knowledge about how to actually *do* anything. By way of comparison, this book is much more open and direct, and it provides a step-by-step plan for study and work.

Like Albertus's *Praxis Spagyrica Philosophica* and his later work, *The Alchemist's Handbook*, *The Path of Alchemy* shows you how to grind medicinal herbs with a mortar and pestle and create tinctures that help to heal and balance mind and body. Certainly this is a practical book, as hands-on as you can hope for. It is also a comforting book. By this I mean that it does not contain hard-to-place symbolism or just hint at things that really could be said directly.

---

1 The book *Praxis Spagyrica Philosophica* was an English translation by Frater Albertus of an eighteenth-century German alchemical manuscript with footnotes regarding alchemical theory and practice, as well as contact information for the now-defunct Paracelsus College.

If you can brew a pot of coffee, you can begin doing the laboratory work detailed here. If you can afford the few dollars needed to buy a copy of *The Path of Alchemy*, you should be able to assemble all of the tools you need to perform experiments. If the fact that the experiments are not complicated suggests to you that they cannot be very revealing, then please hang on for a great ride!

The Path of Alchemy is quite positive and affirmative, but there are a few "no's": no oaths, no secrecy, no gurus, no master, no limits on your imagination and freedom. No guarantees, either, save one: no effort, no result. Making this book is exactly right for today's student—it packs all of the transformational dynamite that Frater Albertus's classic *The Alchemist's Handbook* delivered in 1960. However, unlike that wonderful little book, this revealing book satisfies our culture's need for speed. *The Path of Alchemy* is designed to be useful now, for anyone willing to give a bit of joyful attention and effort.

This book is a tool for personal transformation. The style and format are contemporary, which makes it easier to begin working on your alchemical realization than if you were reading what has previously been available. I say this with the greatest respect for those teachers who have gone before on this path, for without their previous efforts it would not be possible to open wider the doors to the Alchemical Temple.

The author of the book you are now reading owes much to Frater Albertus as well as to other generous teachers, most notably Jean Dubuis.[2] Great teachers intend that those who come after them will accomplish even greater things. As alchemy is the work of evolution, one should not be surprised that changes come one after the other, and with increasing speed.

Alchemy is transformational, healing, balancing. This Great Art has not yet been fully revealed in its implications for planetary harmony. Do you imagine that this book or another one will describe

2 Jean Dubuis is a French alchemist who founded an alchemical school, Les Philosophes des la Nature, which also had an English-language school, the Philosophers of Nature. Both are now defunct, although the written courses are still available in both French and English through Triad Publishing in Winfield, Illinois.

how to change the planet with alchemical healing, or that somehow it is necessary to get all of the presidents, kings, popes, and potentates to embrace an ancient art and science in a modern wrapping?

The legendary Stone of the Philosophers is said to be such in its power and nature that only a few grains are necessary to change a mass of lead into the purest gold. If the potential for such rapid evolution exists in the metallic kingdom, can we imagine that such a power might exist in regard to the human condition?

The culture in much of our planet today is one of increasing information; in fact, it has increased so much that we risk being overloaded to the point that we become lost and detached from what is real. The speed of discovery increases moment by moment, and it seems that the stresses in our lives accelerate at a similar rate. Our families, our countries, and our planet seem to be bursting at the seams with pressure, with no desirable end in sight.

The need for urgency and tenderness in planetary transformation seems necessary when we survey the widespread pain and suffering that is the human condition. There is so much to hope for when we experience true love and friendship, those treasures beyond price, and as we reflect on the beauty of nature expressed in each tender flower, in the awesome grace and power of a lion, in the delicacy of a butterfly, and in the system and order expressed in a crystal grown within the skin of our planet.

The harmony transcribed from the celestial spheres by Beethoven and others, the sculpture and paintings of the master artists, the great dream-stories of Native American shamans, which bring the heights of human aspiration one step closer to earth—each suggests that creative transformation is something that we are inherently skilled enough to accomplish to satisfy our need for spiritual sustenance.

Yet the myriad effects of ignorance, deprivation, disease, and greed bear evidence of our imbalance and suggest that our creative realization is not yet complete. Until such time, the alchemical fire will not be extinguished. The drama of creation, transformation, evolution, and healing will play out in your own heart and mind as you dare to discover your true nature and role in this Great Work. Perhaps then you will become a vehicle for accelerating evolution in the four kingdoms.

I have been very fortunate at every step on my own alchemical journey to have found those generous individuals who were willing and able to help people. Others who had gone before these teachers had helped them, and they in turn continued the chain of good deeds and service. *The Path of Alchemy* is one visible expression of a tradition of care and concern for the well-being of humanity. It is my sincere hope that you will share my fortune, not measured in gold or material accomplishment, but rather in a sense of purpose and of daily revelation and affirmation of the goodness of life and the infusion of hope and purpose.

Carry on, and keep up the good work that you have already begun!

Russell House
Wheaton, Illinois, 2005

ACKNOWLEDGMENTS

Thank you to the many students, friends, and teachers who have made and continue to make alchemy a living tradition. With heartfelt gratitude for all of their efforts, assistance, and insight, thank you to Russell House, Patrice Maleze, Jean Dubuis, and Jack Glass. Special thanks are also sent to Frater Albertus, Hans Nintzel, and Kevin Townley for their foresight in bringing alchemy into the modern world.

Thank you to Marc Thorner of Thorner Graphics for his assistance in producing much-needed artwork and diagrams, and thanks to Christopher Bilardi of Two Ravens Communications and Paul Bowersox for their editorial review and invaluable suggestions, which greatly improved the text.

I would also like to thank two very special women who have tolerated all of this nonsense for so long: Sue House, president of Triad Publishing, who in her own right can be called the "mother of American alchemy," and my wife, Andrea Nerozzi, who made sure I had the time needed to do the work and that I didn't leave any fires unattended.

INTRODUCTION

The writing of *The Path of Alchemy* has been a long and interesting journey. Many of its readers will recognize material from several online articles of mine that have become standard reading on the Internet since their posting in the late 1990s. The articles forming the core of the technical section were originally written at the request of *Ariadne's Web*, a journal well known among students of Rosicrucianism, Martinism, the Knights Templar, and similar initiatic lines of the Western esoteric traditions. Initially, only one article was to be produced, but the decision came quickly to create a trilogy and give a complete and thorough overview, no matter how brief, on the basics of plant alchemy—or more accurately, spagyrics.

What was thought of as being a short course on plant alchemy for a small audience quickly became a phenomenon. The articles were reprinted in *The Rosicrucian Beacon*, the official publication of the Rosicrucian Order (AMORC) for its British and English-speaking European and African members, over several issues in 1998. AMORC's Grand Lodge of the Netherlands published the articles in translation from 2000 to 2001 in its journal *De Roos*, or *The Rose*. For many devoted, even longtime students of alchemy, these three articles have done more to assist them on their practical paths than most of the material that had been around for decades.

Many students of alchemy quickly find themselves limited by the amount of available material in print on practical laboratory techniques. While there is a great deal more available as of this writing than when these articles were initially written, aspiring alchemists still find themselves struggling with two principal texts: *The Alchemist's Handbook*, by Frater Albertus, and *The Practical Handbook of Plant Alchemy*, by Manfred Junius. Both books are written by masters of the art and explain a great deal in clear and concise language. However, students who have read both books will quickly realize that at points Albertus gives his reader not enough information, while Junius gives too much. Both authors require laboratory equipment to do the work, and they both leave out some simple yet very powerful experiments that can be done with little more than kitchen supplies. *The Path of Alchemy* seems to walk the thin middle ground between these giants, and like Baby Bear's porridge, it is "just right" in the information department.

In addition to the familiar text, new illustrations make the operations clear to the first-time student. Meditations and visualizations are clearly articulated so that these often difficult and highly symbolic subjects can have meaning on the practical as well as spiritual level. Each chapter has a summary, assignments, and meditative practices specific to the material in that chapter.

It is to Russell House that I owe a great debt of gratitude, as his generous assistance helped make much of this material more precise and practical on its initial writing. Russell and his wife, Sue, are well known to students of alchemy, as they were central figures in the now-defunct alchemical-Qabalistic organization the Philosophers of Nature (PON).[1] The Philosophers of Nature was started in France in 1978 by Jean Dubuis, a high-ranking member of the French jurisdiction of AMORC and its related Martinist organization, the Traditional Martinist Order (TMO). As a result of his fame in alchemical research with emphasis on the Flamel Path, Dubuis was interviewed for the BBC documentary *Discovering the Real World of Harry Potter* (2002),[2] and he is legendary for having the largest Martinist lodge

---

1 In 2000, Russ and Sue House were featured on the A&E/History Channel documentary *Alchemy: The Search for Science*.

2 Available through Questar, Inc., P.O. Box 11345, Chicago, IL 60611; 1-800-544-8422; www.questar1.com.

(*heptad*) in Paris in the 1970s, with two hundred members. The highest class of about fifty were involved in practical works of theurgy, or ceremonial magic, similar to those undertaken by Martinez Pasquelez more than two hundred years earlier. They were also heavily influenced by *The Cosmic Doctrine*, written by Dion Fortune.

Dubuis left his Rosicrucian and Martinist affiliations to pursue and promote what he called the "dis-occultising" of esotericism. Feeling that much of what was occurring in European circles was simply secrecy for the sake of secrecy, he felt that it no longer served any purpose.

This book appears with much the same spirit, in that it was written to make as clear as possible the basic methods of alchemy for those who desire to learn. All is stated, there are no blinds, and it holds nothing back. The reason for this is simple—each must be responsible for his or her own "Becoming." Since no one can do the work for another, we all must have access to methods and techniques that will help us on our personal Path of Return.

Alchemy is often referred to as "women's work and child's play," in that it involves many of the same skills and temperatures (for plant work, anyway) found in cooking. One needs an open and joyous heart—as a child at play—when undertaking the work. However, I would be remiss if I did not include some safety guidelines, particularly for those who wish to go on to work with minerals. Remember, safety is first, and not an option.

1. Check your local ordinances and state guidelines to see what is permissible in your area when working with chemicals or distilling wine.

2. Read all directions for suggested experiments several times before conducting the actual experiment. Visualize the process, write it out, and be familiar with each step required.

3. Do not use the same tools or cookware for eating that you use for alchemical experiments.

4. Fire is always a potential hazard. Keep a fire extinguisher or fire blanket nearby and know how to use them in case you ever need to. Keep a large box of baking soda on hand should an alcohol spill catch fire and need to be smothered.

While the temperatures you will work with are very low, safety is a habit that is very important—one that will carry over into any work you might want to perform with minerals, where the potential for injury or harm is dramatically more significant.

Several well-intended critics have pointed out that some of the earlier materials produced failed to distinguish between spagyrics and alchemy; these critics claimed that they share common theory and methods but in fact are two different areas of work. Spagyrics is really a part of alchemy, and in its most basic form is concerned with healing the body, similar in fashion to homeopathy. Unlike alchemy, however, it requires no special inner state on the part of the operator and, in this manner, functions much like the "natural magic" of the Renaissance philosophers. Dubuis put it this way:

> Spagyrics essentially deals with bodily health. It is not an initiatory pursuit, whereas alchemy is the medicine of the "soul" and its true goal is initiatory. Spagyric operations, particularly, operations of the vegetable kingdom, do not require a specific state from the operator. The link between work-matter and operator is weak. On the contrary, in alchemy, the bonding between matter and operator is very strong, and no one can transmute anything if he hasn't transmuted himself first. In alchemy, the psychic quality of the operator is essential. . . . There is another important difference. . . . Spagyrics purifies the vessel in order to eliminate the toxic part and then creates in the body a state of resonance that increases the level of energy considerably. Alchemy also purifies matter and its energies but in addition—and this is the essential difference—it accelerates the evolution of matter.[3]

However, this point does give room for thought. If the proper attitude is not essential but spagyrics still produces wondrous results,

---

3 Jean Dubuis, "Spagyrics," *The Stone* 1, no. 1 (Fall 1990): 4. Back issues of *The Stone* are available through Triad Publishing.

then what if a genuine attitude of heart and evolution is brought to the work? Can spagyric operations become alchemical if the operator brings the proper attitude to them? Given that certain spagyric products are initiatic in nature, the Ens of Paracelsus in particular, some believe that spagyrics as a whole can be initiatic if the proper attitude is applied. It is left to each operator to decide this point. Students of quantum physics will also note the similarity between the statements regarding mineral work, the critical importance of the consciousness of the operator on the outcome, and modern findings on the influence of consciousness at the subatomic level.

It has been my good fortune to know several of the leading lights of modern alchemy. After reading Frater Albertus's work *The Alchemist's Handbook*, I sought to make contact with his Paracelsus Research Society (PRS) in Salt Lake City, Utah. By the time I contacted it in 1986, Albertus was dead and the school was struggling to continue without its founder and leader. I then made plans to attend AMORC's Rose-Croix University classes on alchemy, only to have to cancel them at the last moment. While I hoped to attend the following year, this was not to be. AMORC cancelled the classes, and when they were reinstated, Russ House and Jack Glass were no longer the instructors.

In the early 1990s, *Gnosis*, the leading journal for information on the Western esoteric traditions, carried a small ad for an organization in Colorado called the Philosophers of Nature, working under its parent organization's French name, Les Philosophes des la Nature, with the abbreviation LPN. It advertised itself as a school of traditional French alchemy and Qabala. I contacted the organization but received no reply. Several months later, a flyer for a seminar on alchemy arrived in my mailbox. I had never heard of the presenter and simply filed it away. Soon, another flyer arrived. This one told of a week-long seminar at the Wild Rose Program Center in St. Charles, Illinois, in September 1994. A man I had never heard of, Jean Dubuis, was the main presenter; however, the flyer listed Russ House and Jack Glass as teaching a five-day class, four hours a day, on spagyrics. I sent in my registration, and my life has never been the same since.

A short article on this seminar appeared in *Gnosis* with the title "Pass the Sulphur, Mercury, and Salt Si'l Vous Plait,"[4] at the time making me a minor celebrity among my esoteric colleagues. For those who attended this "summer of alchemical love," it was truly a magical event. Many of esotericism's biggest and best names were present, along with at least a dozen alumni from Albertus's PRS days, including Kevin Townley, the president of LPN's American branch (LPN-USA); Hanz Nintzel, a man whose ability to annoy those around him was only exceeded by his love of alchemy; and Art Kunkin, former editor of the *Los Angeles Free Press*. Nintzel and Kunkin inherited various portions of Israel Regardie's estate when he died in 1985: Nintzel received several large mosaic tables and displays of Egyptian and Hermetic themes made by Regardie, and Kunkin received Regardie's library and alchemical laboratory.

Something not widely known is that Regardie studied alchemy at PRS. This changed his view that alchemy was only a speculative and symbolic study, as he had previously stated in his book *The Philosopher's Stone*. It is also important to note that Regardie injured his lungs during an experiment that went awry and as a result needed to use oxygen later in life. A warning to us all, and good reason to proceed with caution.

While it is easy to lament the passing of old friends, particularly those who are looked to as "the greats" in their field, it is important to remember that alchemy is a very personal path. We learn from others, but must do the work ourselves. The tradition of alchemy is a vital and living one, and it will continue to be so for a long time, as long as human beings seek to understand and unlock the Divine in matter and, as a result, in themselves.

As you proceed through this book, remember to "make haste slowly." A little bit of work done regularly is better than a great deal done quickly and on occasion. Take time to pray and meditate as

---

4 *Gnosis*, Winter 1994–95.

you undertake the experiments described in these pages. Think of this not as a book, but as a conversation with a friend, assisting you in your personal work. Hang a small picture of Thoth, Hermes, Flamel, St. Germain, or some other suitable alchemist in your laboratory and imagine that it is they who are communicating these words to you. Let the meditations sink deep into your consciousness so that there you may awake to find yourself in the company of your Inner Master. May these words bring you closer on your journey, and may each of you know that in your heart, one day, you will *become* the Philosopher's Stone. God bless you.

In the Bonds of Esotericism,

Mark Stavish
Director of Studies
Institute for Hermetic Studies
Wyoming, Pennsylvania
24 July 2004

one

ALCHEMY: AN INTRODUCTION TO THE ROYAL ART

Alchemy, long known for its massive symbolic tomes and metaphorical references to plants, minerals, and various elemental intelligences, is among the most mysterious of mystical arts.

CHAPTER OVERVIEW
- *Why Study Alchemy?*
- *Egypt: The Land of Khem*
- *The Key to All Magic*

Visions of old men in funny hats bent over ovens for hours seeking to turn lead into gold, find the Elixir of Life, or create the Philosopher's Stone are commonplace in the popular imagination as well as in occult circles. However, far from being an ancient pursuit whose goals are obscured through the mists of time, alchemy is very much alive and has much to offer our current age. Alchemy's comprehensiveness can offer us tremendous insight into alternative therapies, new medicines, quantum physics, parapsychology, and the depths of the human mind.

WHY STUDY ALCHEMY?

There are many reasons individuals pursue spiritual paths. Some try to fill a void in their lives that other activities, such as drugs, sex, shopping, and psychoanalytical therapy, are unable to satisfy. Others seek power, fame, and wealth, or maybe something simpler, like finding a new boyfriend or girlfriend. In the end, however, it is happiness that we all seek, regardless of the expression we think it will take when we first begin our journey. Of all the choices we can make in life, only a genuine spiritual practice can offer us the opportunity to discover freedom from spiritual ignorance and material suffering and to develop our positive potential to its fullest.

The art of alchemy is best described by Stanislas Klossowski de Rola in *Alchemy: The Secret Art*, his pictorial book on the Great Work:

> Alchemy is a rainbow bridging the chasm between the earthly and heavenly planes, between matter and spirit. . . . Alchemy, the royal sacerdotal art, also called the hermetic philosophy, conceals, in eso-teric texts and enigmatic emblems, the means of penetrating the very secrets of Nature, Life, and Death, of Unity, Eternity, and Infinity. Viewed in the context of these secrets, that of gold making is, rela-tively speaking, of little consequence: something comparable to the super-powers (*siddhis*) sometimes obtained by Great Yogis, which are sought not after for their own sake, but are important by-products of high spiritual attainment.[1]

In short, alchemy offers us the opportunity to relieve suffering, ignorance, and fear of death through direct experience of the invis-ible worlds and understanding how they relate to the physical world of matter. The alchemical path can bring us peace of mind, a posi-tive outlook on life, and increased vitality and creativity. Most im-portantly, alchemy helps us become better people.

In alchemy, inner transformation is accomplished by using a dual process of transpersonal and technical methods. The transpersonal methods are the meditations, prayers, studies, and inner work that the alchemist undertakes. The technical methods are the physical techniques and preparations the alchemist uses to produce herbal and mineral tinctures, which can be used as ritual aids or medici-nally. This dual approach develops a positive feedback loop in which the action in the lab reinforces meditative practices and meditative practices enhance energy for transforming products in the labora-tory. In the end, the alchemist transforms him or herself by experi-

---

1 Stanislas Klossowski de Rola, *Alchemy: The Secret Art* (London: Thames and Hudson, 1973).

menting with Nature's subtle energies and thereby awakening the Inner Light.

This book will demonstrate in a clear, easy-to-understand, and point-by-point manner the simple techniques of basic alchemy. If you've read even a single book on magic, witchcraft, Wicca, or alternative healing, you already know about half of what you need to be successful! In this book, herbalists will find the means of making tinctures and Elixirs that are considerably more powerful than standard herbal, homeopathic, or flower essences. Wiccans and Neopagans will discover simple, easy-to-use methods of creating magical products utilizing planetary and elemental energies with emphasis on lunar cycles. You can do all of the experiments in this book in a kitchen, using common household appliances if laboratory glassware is unavailable.

If you are a beginning or intermediate student of occultism, consider the following points:

1. Alchemy helps us to understand the fundamental unity of the cosmos and our place in it by weaving together the various occult disciplines into a cohesive whole.

2. Alchemy is ideal for the solo practitioner with limited time who does not have access to, or is reluctant to join, esoteric groups.

3. Alchemical products can be stored—and their ability to induce deeper meditative insights, lucid dreams, and spiritual initiation can be repeated—without any loss in strength or potency.

4. Alchemical products are helpful even if the recipient does not believe in energetic healing, magic, or other forms of esotericism.

THE LAND OF KHEM: WHERE IT ALL BEGAN

Egypt. No other country on earth has been held in such high esteem for so many millennia. Generations of seekers have gone to the portals of her temples to learn the secrets of magic. While many civilizations have possessed religious institutions, no other country has so thoroughly created a culture in which the spiritual world ruled every aspect of daily life than the land of mummies, tombs, gods, and pharaohs.

In Egypt, the gods were ever-present and were so real that to speak of "religion" as we experience it in modern life would be false. The ancient Egyptian language did not have a word for religion as we know it, only magic—and more precisely, magical power. Everything in Egyptian life was classed according to its perceived amount of magical power. Gods rose and fell on it, and humans could rule the gods through it. Egyptian life focused around the ever-present energies of life and how to harness them for now and the afterlife.

Egypt is said to have even given her name to early alchemy, as Egypt is known as the "land of Khem" or the "black earth." While we attribute Egypt with being the home of alchemy and its god Thoth, or Hermes in his Greek incarnation, with being the father of alchemy, other lands have contributed as well. China and India have highly developed alchemical laboratory traditions that have been practiced in unbroken lines since their inception.

It is in the West, however, that we see some of the most fascinating aspects of the Great Art developed. Here, Babylonian, Chaldean, Egyptian, Greek, Hebrew, and Arabic methods were worked side by side. Arab trade most likely also introduced Chinese and Indian methods into the Middle East and, ultimately, Europe. These diverse traditions were amalgamated in an attempt to discover the process for creating the Philosopher's Stone, or the Stone of the Wise.

Said to confer the ability to transmute base metals into gold, prolong life, and cure all diseases, the Philosopher's Stone was a mineral creation made most famous by the fourteenth-century French alchemist Nicholas Flamel and his wife, Perenelle. With it, it is said, they created the Elixir of Immortality and were seen alive three hundred years after their recorded deaths. While the kind of mineral work the Flamels undertook is beyond the scope of this text, a few simple experiments with the considerably easier and less dangerous herbal work of alchemy will demonstrate why many thought these extraordinary claims about the Flamels to be true.

This idea of a Stone—or of an actual physical object as a means of bringing about dramatic changes in the health and, above all, the spiritual consciousness of an individual—is the basis for most experiments in all three kingdoms the alchemist will progressively work through. Anyone familiar with the idea of talismans, or ritually charging objects such as liquids or metals for a specific purpose, already has a sense of how an alchemical tincture or Stone functions.

THE KEY OF ALL MAGIC: SEPARATING THE GROSS FROM THE SUBTLE

Like magic, alchemy seeks to demonstrate the reality of cosmic truths in the daily life of its practitioners. While a nominal amount of Qabala and astrology are traditionally studied in concert with practical alchemy, students of any system of magic will quickly see the relationship between magic and alchemy, the most obvious and useful of these links being between what we often call natural magic and the creation of specialized herbal tinctures. *Natural magic* is the use of astrological and planetary cycles in connection with magical or alchemical experiments to direct the greatest amount of psychic energy with the least amount of effort. When applied to the creation of alchemical products from herbs, the process is known as *spagyrics* and is only slightly more complicated than making standard herbal products—the key difference being in the Hermetic practice of "separating the gross from the subtle."

This separation is energetically similar, if not identical, to the processes of banishing and invoking done in ritual magic, preparing tools for consecration, and creating a talisman. In an alchemical product, however, once the process of separating (banishing) and recombining (invoking) is completed, the process will repeat and will continue on its own until the next phase of the work is undertaken. Through the use of simple and well-known astrological and Qabalistic laws, the process of refining the energetic content and structure of an alchemical product, be it herbal or mineral, will continue on its own after the alchemist has initiated the process. This leaves the alchemist time to work on other aspects of his or her development, or other alchemical projects. Once made, the energy of the spagyric product does not dissipate over time, and in some instances it actually increases, unlike the energy of talismans, which must be repeatedly recharged to be of use.

The study of astrology, for the timing of experiments, and the use of esoteric meditation, for the raising of spiritual energy known as the *Secret Fire* (or *kundalini* in yoga), are part of the alchemist's discipline. The alchemist is in essence a mystic, an astrologer, and a magician. This is a critical point, for to attempt to separate out the physical actions of the alchemist without the interior exercises is to reduce alchemy to mundane chemistry. For alchemy to be alchemy, the divine aspect must always be present in the consciousness of the operator. To assist in this critical interior part of alchemy, this book includes extensive meditations and visualizations to assist in building the psychic bridge between the inner and outer worlds of the aspiring alchemist. These meditations are based upon the principles of natural magic, making them simple, direct, easy to practice, and beneficial to anyone regardless of his or her main spiritual path—be it Qabala, Wicca, or Neopaganism.

THE STAGES OF THE GREAT WORK AND ASTROLOGY

The existing works on alchemy suggest that the Great Work, or *Magnum Opus*, of spiritual and physical regeneration consists of seven or twelve stages, which are repeated over and over again until perfection is obtained. These stages are first done in the World of Plants and then in the World of Minerals. Some schools, including that of Paracelsus, propose that work can also be done in the animal realm; however, this idea is often shunned by many practitioners.

The stages are said to represent the ones that Nature herself went through during the beginnings of creation. They are also represented in the cosmos by the twelve signs of the zodiac and in the human organism by the seven major and five minor (for a total of twelve) psychospiritual centers called *chakras* in Sanskrit. These centers are also linked to the endocrine and nervous systems in human beings.

Sign	Physical Organs	Energy	Psychic Center	Alchemical Phase
Aries	Head	Active	Mars	Calcination
Taurus	Neck/Throat	Passive	Venus	Coagulation
Gemini	Shoulders	Active	Mercury	Fixation
Cancer	Lungs/Stomach	Passive	Moon	Dissolution
Leo	Heart	Active	Sun	Digestion
Virgo	Intestines	Passive	Mercury	Distillation
Libra	Hips	Active	Venus	Sublimation
Scorpio	Sexual Organs	Passive	Mars	Separation
Sagittarius	Thighs	Active	Jupiter	Incineration
Capricorn	Knees	Passive	Saturn	Fermentation
Aquarius	Ankles	Active	Saturn	Multiplication
Pisces	Feet	Passive	Jupiter	Projection

This linking of the stages of alchemy to the zodiac, as well as to the organs of the human body, was part of everyday medical practices during the Middle Ages and Renaissance. However, alchemy takes the associations one step further, in that they are applied not only to the physical body but to the energetic or etheric body as well. It is the etheric body that alchemical products seek to work on, and like acupuncture or homeopathy, this is what gives alchemy its healing powers. However, some alchemical products can also work on the psychic or astral body. These are often mineral products, and they give access to deep levels of spiritual initiation. Fortunately, as we will outline, there are some herbal products as well that can provide initiatic experiences, and these are also easy to produce.

By creating a product that acts on an organ, we can address physical health directly; this is the most basic feature of medical astrology.

However, acting on a particular energy allows us to affect the etheric or energy body as well as the physical body. An alchemical product also acts through a specific psychic center and stimulates the psychic body, the etheric body, and the physical body with increased energy. As the energy circulates throughout the etheric energy system and the physical body through the bloodstream, all twelve phases of the alchemical process are replicated within the body itself, as well as in the etheric and astral bodies to varying degrees.

In this way, our physical, etheric, and psychic bodies become the living laboratories of the alchemical work. In and through them, we experience the results of our labors, and through intuition, we can be guided during the most difficult stages of the work.

QABALA AND ALCHEMY: A FOOL'S JOURNEY

Qabala provides many keys to understanding alchemy, particularly its different methods, as well as keys to interpreting the various symbols encountered. Many of these symbols are seen in books and manuscripts and are used as metaphors to both veil and reveal the secrets they contain. Through dreams, meditations, and spontaneous insights, past alchemists were able to understand the documents they were using, as well as interpret them for others. It is not uncommon to enter into alchemical gardens or palaces in one's dreams after undertaking this practice. Qabala helps us to better understand the meanings of the symbols we may encounter.

Among the most useful of Qabalistic tools is the Tree of Life. Through its simple yet profound structure, the entire cosmos can be explained and understood. Relationships are made clear, and all manner of mental, physical, and psychological illness can be diagnosed and resolved. Ignorance can be turned into Light, and death into life. While many students of Qabala spend years studying the Tree of Life and its intricate symbols, alchemists (who may not wish to be Qabalists as well) can utilize only its most basic components to guide them along the Path of Return.

The *Path of Return* is the way whereby each human soul goes from gross ignorance to Illumination—and the various phases, challenges, and encounters along the way. This path starts in the material world in which we live and takes our consciousness to the heights of perfect wisdom, compassion, and power. However, unlike some systems that seek to escape from matter and see it as evil, alchemy recognizes the inherent energy and power in matter and uses it for the journey. Alchemy says that we are to perfect ourselves through the challenges material life offers us, not run from them into a fantasy land of "spiritual perfection" that is little more than a fear of life itself.

This premature return to the Invisible Worlds—without first having learned to master material life, and thereby master ourselves—is symbolized in the tarot as the Lightning-Struck Tower. Return without wisdom is the real journey of the Fool, but to return with wisdom, power, and Illumination is to be the Magician—the co-creator with the cosmos. This is the tarot equivalent of the alchemist, a Magus who understands, uses, and directs the forces of consciousness, energy, and matter and realizes that they are One.

Just as astrology helps us to understand the influence of cycles on energy and matter without having to become astrologers, Qabala helps the aspiring alchemical adept to understand the influence of symbols without having to become a full-fledged Qabalist. However, the unique synthesis that alchemy offers often allows students to become far more skilled in all three areas of study than they would have thought possible had an attempt been made to study them independently. The reason for this is simple: alchemy is experientially oriented; thus, what we learn, we learn through experience and not memorization.

QABALA 101: USING THE TREE OF LIFE WITH ALCHEMY

The single greatest advantage to using the Tree of Life in connection with alchemy is that it allows for a very neat and practical "filing cabinet" for ideas. Everything the alchemist, Qabalist, or astrologer might encounter can find its place on the Tree of Life, and through the Tree, map its relationship to every other phenomena—mental, physical, or psychic—that might or could possibly occur. However, like a filing cabinet or computer in the material world, we don't need to know how everything works in order to take advantage of its benefits.

The second most important aspect to using the Tree of Life is that it describes the creation of the universe, and therefore everything in it, in a simple and direct manner from the perspective of consciousness, then energy, and finally matter.

In Qabala (and alchemy), creation takes place when the divine mind of God, the Absolute, or in Hebrew the *Ain Soph Aur* (Limitless Light), through a series of expansions and contractions, establishes the boundaries of creation, as follows:

1. The first world, *Atziluth*, is the most subtle and is closest to the original state of nonexistence. This is called the World of Fire, because of the lively, undefined, and almost uncontrollable nature of fire.

2. Next is *Briah*, the World of Archetypes, or forms as our human mind can grasp them. It is symbolized as the World of Air and acts as a barrier world between the extremes of the World of Fire preceding it and the World of Water following it.

3. *Yetzirah*, or the World of Water, is the highly psychic and emotionally charged world immediately behind the veil of material existence.

4. *Assiah*, the World of Action, is also known as the World of Earth, because of the solid, concrete nature of material life. This world contains physical matter as well as the subtle energy web, or etheric energy, forming physical life, such as the meridians in acupuncture or ley lines in dowsing.

In basic alchemy, plants are used to affect the quality and quantity of energy flow through the World of Earth (the physical world) and its etheric structure and the World of Water (the astral world). Only mineral alchemy can permanently affect the World of Air, allowing access to the World of Fire, but that is beyond the scope of this text.

Creation occurs in increasingly dense levels of energy-matter, from the subtlest, Fire, to the densest, Earth. Within this context of increasing density, there also arises a series of ten planes or levels of consciousness known as *Sephiroth*, or spheres of being. Each sphere is a self-contained world that relates to other self-contained worlds. In this way, they can be understood as countries with their own inhabitants, customs, laws, and languages, but they are also connected to the other "countries" that form the Tree of Life.

These spheres appear on the Tree in the following pattern: unity, reflection, polarity, reflection, polarity, unity, reflection, polarity, unity, and finally materialization. This basic idea of unity, polarity, and synthesis is the basis of Qabalistic and alchemical practices and is derived from the observation of Nature.

Each world reflects to a denser or subtler degree the one before or after it. Each Sephirah is a reflection, in part, of what precedes or follows it. However, since each reflection is only partial, or slightly distorted, each sphere takes on its own unique characteristics. Only the four spheres composing what Qabalists call the "Middle Pillar" have the ability to harmonize or reflect in total all of the energies of creation, on some level. It is on these spheres that the alchemist focuses his or her attention in order to create alchemical products that change consciousness.

The effects of this awakening will take some time for the consciousness of the individual to adjust to, and they are not limited to the nonphysical realms. The physical body, albeit to a lesser degree, is also changed and improved in its functioning, constituting a genuine "rebirth" on several levels. However, it is up to the mind, or sense of "I," of the individual to cooperate with this influx of power if more permanent changes in consciousness are to take place.

The use of the Tree of Life has been both a blessing and a curse for modern esotericism. When understood, the Tree offers a complete

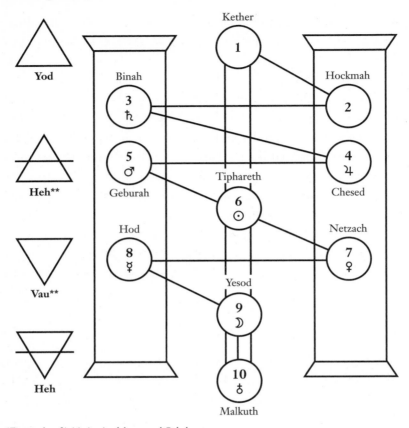

Kether

Yod

Binah

Hockmah

Heh**

Geburah

Tiphareth

Chesed

Hod

Netzach

Vau**

Yesod

Heh

Malkuth

*First paths of initiation in alchemy and Qabala
**The order of the elements on the Tree according to alchemy

*Tree of Life**

and working model of creation on both the microcosmic and macro-cosmic scales. However, where many fail is on the personal level. The ability to apply the often very general information of the Tree to the personal experiences of the initiate when he or she deals with physi-ological phenomena is profoundly lacking in modern esoteric circles. The reasons for this are several: first, many modern esotericists sim-ply repeat what they have learned without experiencing whether or not it is true on a personal level; second, the language of Qabala is multileveled, with the same word having several meanings, and thus many who are using the words don't know what they actually mean or on what levels they may be interpreted; third, the diagram of the Tree is simply too neat and compartmentalized, and many Qabalists are unable to adapt to the fact that interior reality is much more flexible than the Tree allows when applied to the two-dimensional page or illustration.

To help resolve these problems in the transmission of knowledge, only information that has a relationship to the experience of the author or others with whom he has discussed this topic will be included here. Theory will be stated as theory, and experience as experience. The meanings of common Qabalistic words will be defined, and redefined, to keep the communication clear and direct. An extensive use of confusing and somewhat irrelevant god-forms, references to mythology, and cosmology unconnected to personal experience will be avoided.

CONCLUSION

Anything worth doing takes time and effort; spiritual studies are no different in this regard. Just as people must discover for themselves which path is best for them, they must also ask if they are getting the "return on their investment" that they initially sought. Few systems of development are as mentally, physically, and spiritually rewarding as the alchemical path. Through it, the entire corpus of Western esoteric philosophy and occult practices can be synthesized, understood, and, most importantly, *effectively applied*. Like any genuine path of spiritual initiation, alchemy is a truly solitary path. We may meet with other alchemists, work with them on occasion, and learn from each other, but the true work is done alone in our laboratories and within our hearts. No one can open nor bar the gateway for us, and all who simply enter onto the path of alchemy will be better off for it than if they had never started.

Dare to practice alchemy—because it works!

KEY POINTS

- Basic alchemy can be successfully studied and applied by anyone who can follow a simple cooking recipe.

- All of the experiments in *The Path of Alchemy* can be done using common household appliances if laboratory glassware is unavailable.

- Alchemy is one of the few occult arts and sciences that is objective in its results.

- Tinctures, Elixirs, and other products increase their potency over time.

- Alchemical products can bring healing in the physical, etheric, and psychic realms.

- True alchemy is about interior growth or initiation. Successful alchemical experiments bring Illumination and spiritual growth.

- Alchemy incorporates the disciplines of astrology and Qabala into itself to form an organic whole, making these areas of study easier to learn and apply.

- Alchemy offers a tremendous "return on investment" for the time involved, given the experiences it can bring.

GENERAL ASSIGNMENTS FOR CHAPTER ONE

- Obtain one or more notebooks to use as you study, or use a large three-ring binder with separators for the various sections. Suggested subject headings: Alchemical Theory, Astrology, Meditations, Outline of Experiments, Qabala, Lab Work. As you progress, other topics may occur to you, as well as a means of cross-referencing between sections. However, obtaining and setting up your notebook(s) is fine for now.

- Reread this chapter and make a list of any concepts that are unclear to you. Keep this list for future reference as you read the remainder of the book and perform the various meditations and experiments.

- Go to a local university library, or online, and look up the following articles in *The Encyclopedia of Religion*, edited by Mircea Eliade: alchemy, Hermeticism, astrology, Qabala, and initiation. Make or print copies for your notebook.

- Copy the chart and diagram in this chapter into your notebook under the appropriate headings.

- Reflect on what it is you want out of your practice of alchemy. What is your motivation for undertaking this work? How will you know when you have achieved it? Write down your answers to these questions in your notebook.

two

BASIC SPAGYRICS

THE THREE ESSENTIALS: SULPHUR, SALT, AND MERCURY

Alchemy sees Nature as powerful, intelligent, and creative—but slow moving in her evolution of self-consciousness. By carefully observing and imitating Nature's methods, the alchemist is able to speed up the process of inner and outer evolution through the three realms of mineral, plant, and animal without violating any of Nature's laws. For example, left to herself, Nature might take several million years to turn vegetable matter into oil, tar, coal, and finally a diamond. While this is fine for Nature, whose lifespan is eternal, for a human being with a limited amount of time on earth, such a process of waiting is impractical, and the human must obtain speedier methods if a diamond is desired for certain alchemical or Qabalistic practices. Even if it is not a diamond that we need but a tincture for healing purposes, we do not wait for a tree to fall and be burrowed out to form a natural chalice and then wait for the rain and wind to blow the right leaves into it, creating a natural medicine that we then have to wander through the forest to find. Instead we pick our herbs, soak them, strain them, and drink our tea when it is done. The process is the same, only quicker and more efficient.

For the aspiring alchemist, the majority of work will take place in the plant kingdom, as the plants worked with are nontoxic, the temperatures used are low, and the work carries the same technical risks as making dinner on a stovetop. If you can boil water, you can do plant alchemy.

In alchemy, everything is composed of three parts: sulphur (soul or individualized essence), mercury (life force), and salt (physical body). It is the work of the alchemist to separate and recombine these three basic principles as often as necessary until they are in perfect proportion and harmony with each other. When this harmony is achieved, the creation of a "Stone," or physical object used in the physical and spiritual transformation of the alchemist, will result. Remember, the plant carries all that it needs to evolve, although the process, if left to nature, will be slow moving. Alchemists have a limited lifespan compared to the substances they work with; they seek to speed up the process of evolution in the plants and minerals they utilize and, in doing so, speed up their own evolution as well. This recognition of physical mortality, combined with the length of time needed to accomplish the Great Work, as it is called, led many alchemists to seek the Elixir of Life so that by extending their lifespan they could complete the task they had assigned themselves.

When working with plants, the physical body of the plant itself is the salt, its essential oils are the sulphur, and alcohol (and occasionally water) is the mercury. Thus, the aspiring alchemist seeks to separate these three parts and recombine them, giving rise to the word used by Paracelsus, *spagyrics* (pronounced "spah-jir-iks"). *Spagyrics* is Greek for "separate and recombine" and is the term given to plant work, or the Lesser Circulation. The Greater Circulation consists of metallic and mineral work; its process follows the same principles as plant work, and it is generally undertaken only after a certain degree of plant mastery has been attained.

THE THREE ESSENTIALS AND THE ELEMENTS

Students familiar with the concept of the elements, or the foundational forces that give rise to creation, will find that the concepts represented by sulphur, mercury, and salt are already known to them, only under a different name. In alchemy, just as in Wicca, Neopaganism, or Qabala, we use the four elements to explain the relationships between energy and matter. These four elements are the foundation for all experiences, expressions of consciousness, and material manifestation. They exist on several levels, giving personal and impersonal expressions of their nature. Alchemy helps us to identify these levels and, in doing so, to achieve our goals.

Fire—In impersonal terms, fire is pure energy. Imagine it as an intense radiating sensation of heat that penetrates everything and transforms it. In personal terms, imagine fire as our spiritual seed, our drive toward the realization of self.

Air—In impersonal terms, imagine air as all things gaseous, expansive, and cohesive. Air is the Cosmic Mind in action, and it is the laws that the alchemist learns so that he or she can manipulate the elements within and without in order to create the Philosopher's Stone. In personal terms, imagine air as the theoretical framework of ideas and images that make accessible the transforming yet seemingly chaotic and dangerous energy of fire.

Water—In impersonal terms, imagine water as all things liquid. Energy is transferred in a liquid state, be it water, rain, blood, hormones, or sexual fluids. Water is the practical means of expressing the energy of fire after it has been transferred by air, just as water ascends and descends through evaporation. In personal terms, imagine elemental water as your personal bodily fluids, and also as the emotions that give force and energy to ideas, making them manifest materially.

Earth—In impersonal terms, imagine elemental earth as all solid matter, even subatomic matter, and the elements. Earth is the etheric structure or invisible net of energy that gives rise to physical form, as well as being the actual form itself. In personal terms, imagine earth as all things material and solid, your physical body, your etheric body, and things in your life.

However, the elements do not exist in a vacuum. They are united in their common source, or Spirit, symbolized by an eight-spoked wheel. This Spirit is a primordial form of energy-consciousness that is utilized in magical rituals as well as in alchemy. Spirit expresses itself in two forms: one active, the other passive. The active energies of Spirit give rise to the so-called "active" elements of fire and air, while the passive aspects of Spirit give rise to the "passive" elements of water and earth. Fire and air are called active because they are highly mobile, unpredictable, and erratic at times. Water and earth are called passive because they are dominated by other forces and move only when acted upon.

These same basic ideas exist in alchemy and demonstrate the fundamental unity of Nature that underlies all alchemical and magical work. According to alchemical cosmology, all of creation arises from a fundamental source of energy and consciousness known as Chaos. This vast unmanifest, void of any form, gives rise to two primary forms of expression: one active, or energy, and the other passive, or matter. These correspond identically to the ideas of active and passive Spirit energy just described, which are used in modern Qabalistic rituals. These two forms of fundamental energy, active and passive, then give rise to subdivisions within themselves, forming the four elements as we know them. These elements then recombine to create the three essentials of alchemy. Fire and air combine to form the self-arising consciousness of sulphur; earth and water combine to form the material world and its etheric matrix, or salt; and air and water combine to form mercury, the medium that allows energy and matter to communicate with each other. Finally, it is through the alchemist's manipulation of these three essentials, separating them back into their principal parts and reassembling them, that he or she may undertake the alchemical work and achieve the Philosopher's Stone.

"*Solve et coagula*," meaning "separate and recombine," is a term you will hear repeatedly in alchemical work, and it is the key to all occult work. Alchemists are constantly separating and recombining the

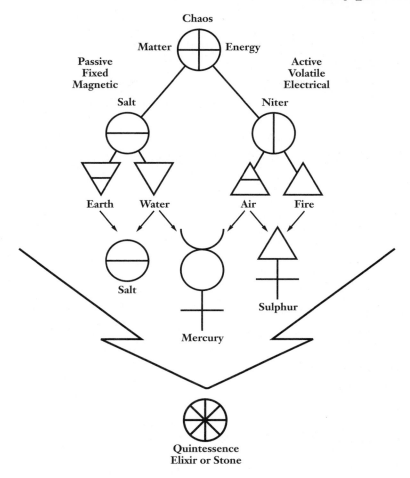

Prima Materia

various essentials and elements of plants, minerals, and, more importantly, themselves, to understand Nature's hidden laws and how they work. Students of tarot see these words emblazoned on the arms of the Devil in the Wirth and Waite decks as well as other tarot decks derived from Qabalistic and alchemical symbolism. It is good to write this motto down on a card and place it where you can easily see it while you are doing your alchemical work. Just as the muscles of the human body grow stronger through the process of breaking down

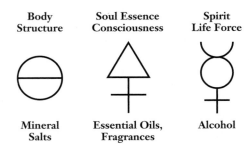

Body Structure	Soul Essence Consciousness	Spirit Life Force
Mineral Salts	Essential Oils, Fragrances	Alcohol

The Three Essentials—Salt, Mercury, and Sulphur

and building up, so do the powers of alchemical products grow more potent through an identical cycle of activity. This process is so fundamental to alchemy, and to the plant experiments outlined here in particular, that you should spend a considerable amount of time meditating on the ideas presented here.

While we can gain much from the theoretical study of spagyrics, only in the actual conducting of experiments will we attain any meaningful degree of insight and growth. For this reason, the following experiments allow would-be alchemists to try it for themselves without a heavy investment in laboratory equipment during their trial period. The methods given and the time for completion reflect this simple, low-tech approach. However, with the proper glassware and heat source, you can dramatically reduce the time required.

EXPERIMENTS FOR THE BEGINNING STUDENT OF THE ART

The production of a spagyric, or plant tincture, is the first and easiest of all operations. It requires no special equipment and can be done by anyone anywhere, needing only patience and perseverance as its primary tools. Here is an example of a tincture made from lemon balm (*Melissa officinalis*), although any plant can be used. You must research plant toxicity prior to working with or ingesting any plant, herb, or part thereof. While often the entire plant can be consumed, in some instances there are plants whose leaves and seeds are safe but whose roots are toxic. Even though the herbs most commonly used are nontoxic, always check to make sure that the plant you are working with is safe to ingest and that you will not have any allergic reactions to working with it.

For each operation, you will need one ounce of dried herb. Unless otherwise stated, the bulk herb will consist of mostly leaves, some stem, and occasionally the roots of the plant. If you are unsure as to the content, either ask the herbalist you are purchasing it from or grow your own and pick it yourself. By growing your own herbs, you will know positively the identity of the plant. While very few people die each year from plant misidentification while wildcrafting (picking plants in the wild), it does one no good to chance being among those dozen or so who do make a fatal error. Be safe: buy it dried or grow it yourself from a well-identified seed or seedling purchased from a reputable supplier.

If dried herbs are not available, fresh plants may be substituted. Alchemists have personal preferences as to when and where to use fresh versus dried plants. Experience will help you sort this out later on. For this experiment, either will suffice.

In addition, you will need 4 to 8 ounces of pure grain alcohol. In some states, purchasing grain alcohol is illegal, and in others, very strong 190 proof, or 95% pure, alcohol is available. The more common 180 proof is sufficient and is often used in plant work for beginners. If neither of these is available, you can substitute vodka or distill alcohol from red wine or strong brandy. (**Note:** Distilling alcohol from wine may also be illegal in some states. Check if you think this may be a problem.)

You will need a wide-mouthed jar, such as one used in canning, along with its lid, plastic food wrap, aluminum foil, and a fine-mesh plastic filter, or coffee filters and a funnel. A mortar and pestle are optional but desirable. A coffee grinder is also helpful.

Checklist

- 1 ounce of dried or fresh herb.
- 4 to 8 ounces of 180- or 190-proof alcohol (substitute vodka or distilled wine or brandy if not available).
- Wide-mouthed canning jar and lid.
- Plastic food wrap for sealing the lid.
- Aluminum foil for wrapping when completed.
- Fine-mesh plastic filter, or coffee filters and funnel.
- Mortar and pestle and/or clean coffee grinder.

Suggested plants and their ruling planets

- The plants you should have are horsetail (Saturn), lemon balm (Jupiter), basil (Mars), eyebright (Sun), lady's mantle (Venus), fennel (Mercury), and watercress (Moon). An additional plant to have is sundew, especially for traveling, as it is said to contain the powers of all seven planets and thereby reduces the number of tinctures you will need to carry with you.

Day	Planet	Power	Physical Organ	Symbol	Herb	Official Name
Saturday	Saturn	Stability	Spleen	♄	Horsetail	*Equisetum arvense*
Sunday	Sun	Self-awareness	Heart	☉	Eyebright	*Euphrasia officinalis*
Monday	Moon	Psychic Development	Brain or Brain Stem	☽	Watercress	*Nasturtium officinale*
Tuesday	Mars	Energy	Gall	♂	Basil	*Ocimum basilicum*
Wednesday	Mercury	Initiation and Communication	Throat/Thyroid	☿	Fennel	*Foeniculum vulgare*
Thursday	Jupiter	Assimilation	Lungs or Stomach	♃	Lemon Balm	*Melissa officinalis*
Friday	Venus	Harmony	Kidneys	♀	Lady's Mantle	*Alchemilla vulgaris*

BASIC SPAGYRIC TINCTURE

1. Read all instructions that follow several times and familiarize yourself with each step that you need to undertake. Remember: Safety first whenever working with spagyric or alchemical experiments or products!

2. Begin the operation in the planetary hour of the ruling planet of the herb. While planetary hours come several times a day for each planet, the first, and often easiest, begins within a few minutes of sunrise on the day of the ruling planet. Since *Melissa* is ruled by Jupiter, and Jupiter rules Thursday, the first planetary hour of Jupiter would occur immediately after sunrise on Thursday.

3. Start with a prayer to God that the mysteries may be revealed to you and your place in the universe restored. Spend a few minutes on this, and do not rush through it. This sets up your entire reason for undertaking this practice and is the intention, or act of will, that sets everything in motion. It is this initial prayer that separates your experiments from "vulgar chemistry" and makes them something spiritual.

4. Take the herb and begin grinding it by hand in small quantities in the mortar and pestle. Make as fine a powder as possible, focusing on the idea that you are releasing the divine power in the herb as well as within yourself through the work. If you do not have enough time to grind all of the herb by hand, or you have a part that is too tough, such as a seed or root, then grind it partially in the coffee grinder. It is important that you spend time with the herb and keep it in physical contact with you so that it may receive beneficial contact with your energy field or aura. If you must grind it entirely by machine, then place it in the mortar afterward and grind it with the pestle anyhow, focusing on developing the energetic relationship between yourself, the herb, the planet ruling it, and the planet's counterparts in your psyche and body.

5. When the powder is finished, place it in the jar and pour the grain alcohol over the herb until it is saturated with fluid; then add an additional amount equal to what is in the container (two to four "fingers"). The jar should not be more than one-half to two-thirds full of fluid at most, as room will be needed for expansion as the contents heat during the maceration process. The fluid inside will evaporate as it heats and then condense, as it is not capable of escaping. This will cause the fluid to get darker with each passing day. This coloration, or tincturing, is the extraction of the sulphur (soul property) from the salt (physical plant matter) by the mercury (alcohol medium).

6. Cover the mouth of the jar with plastic wrap prior to sealing it tightly with the lid so that neither the fluid nor its vapor touch any metal.

7. Wrap the jar in foil to prevent exposure to light, and place it somewhere warm.

8. Shake it vigorously once or twice a day. Continue this process for seven to fourteen days, until the color of the tincture is dark. However, it is not uncommon to allow the tincture to sit for forty days, an "alchemical month."

That's it: seven steps and you have begun the process of making a basic spagyric tincture that will be helpful to you physically and spiritually. But remember, this is your "philosophical child" and must be treated with love and respect. Each time you handle it, for inspection, for shaking, or in any fashion, remember that it is a physical representation of your soul-personality. Treat it no differently than you would treat a small animal, a child, or a houseguest. As you separate the sulphur from the murky sludge of the herbal mass, so are you separating your soul from the constraints of physical life and incarnation. Just as the soul of the plant is what distinguishes it from other plants, so your soul, your consciousness, and your inner impulse to realize your self is what separates you from other human beings.

In this manner, it is the soul of the alchemist that impacts and changes the soul of the plant in the tincture. It is the attitude of the operator, more than the process itself, that makes alchemy divine. This attitude is literally transferred to the matter being acted upon, just as if it were a patient receiving magnetic or spiritual healing. When the final product is then consumed, we are taking into ourselves a veritable consumable talisman—like that which is suggested by the Christian Mass—through which our body (salt) and blood (mercury) are regenerated, to receive the spiritual power of the plant (sulphur).

Each time we repeat the process of "solve et coagula," we are regenerated by minute degrees and brought closer to perfection.

What to Do When the Tincture Is Complete

After the color of the liquid is sufficiently dark, pour it into a clean jar that can be sealed. Be careful to strain or filter the tincture through either a plastic fine-mesh strainer or coffee filters placed inside a funnel. To maximize your efforts, press the remaining fluid from the plant matter through the screen over the filter-lined funnel. The filter will catch any plant matter or particles that might be forced through the strainer and prevent them from mixing in with the tincture. On close examination under light, you will see that some small amount of fine, sandlike particles will flow through with the tincture, but for now we can ignore them rather than replace our commercial over-the-counter coffee filters with laboratory-grade paper filters. Right now, our concern is to separate the fluid from the solid matter as best we can. For the purposes of getting started and getting results that will encourage us to move into more complex areas of alchemical work, this will be sufficient.

This tincture now contains the sulphur (essential oils, waxes, and vegetable fats) and the mercury (alcohol and some water) of the lemon balm. This tincture is identical to any basic herbal product you could make or purchase in a grocery or health-food store. What will transform it into a genuine spagyric, or herbal alchemical product, is the addition of the process of "coagula." We have separated the plant soul, or sulphur, from the body, or salt. That is the process of "solve," or dissolution. Now, we must add the two together again in some form. But for the resurrection of the plant to be complete, its body, or salt, must be purified and made ready to receive the increase in energy. To do this, we use the alchemist's chief tool—fire. Fire is the energetic expression of the universe. Of the four elements common to Wicca, Neopaganism, Qabala, and Hermeticism, fire is the only one that can completely transform and regenerate. This process is known as *calcination*, and it turns the wet, dark matter of the plant into a white or grayish white powder ready for use in the next step of the process.

CALCINATION

Up until now, the process of making tinctures has been relatively safe and has not involved an open flame. While alcohol burns at a low temperature, it is important to follow some simple safety guidelines when calcinating herbal materials so that you may avoid any injuries or damage to property.

Equipment Needed
- Pyrex bowl or container, preferably with a lid.
- Metal rod for stirring the mass to turn the fire so it keeps burning.
- Heatproof or fireproof surface to rest the bowl on while the plant matter is burning.
- Hot pads or gloves to handle the container when the process is completed.
- Mortar and pestle.
- Additional alcohol for repeating the process.
- Plastic or metal scoop for handling the cool ashes.
- Container that can be tightly sealed to place the ash in after the process is completed.

Safety Tips

To protect against sudden changes in wind that may cause the flames to flare up when initially started, it is common to calcine in a barbecue, brick fireplace, or cinder-block fire pit, like those often used to cook outdoors in the spring and summer. Some alchemists calcine in the less-populated areas of public parks where fire pits and cooking areas are common. It is also a good idea to keep your container's lid handy in case you need to smother the flames.

In the rare and unusual event that the burning material actually spills, do not panic. Simply smother it with baking soda, sand, a large wet towel, or a fire extinguisher. A panic attack under these circumstances is far more dangerous than the size or heat of the actual fire if you are working in one of the fire-resistant or fireproof areas mentioned.

The Calcining Process

1. Read the entire set of instructions several times before proceeding.

2. Take the plant mass, or *feces* (also called the *caput mortuum*, or "dead head"), and ignite it in a heat-resistant container. This is best done outside, as the burning will produce a great deal of smoke. For this operation, a large, deep glass container used for baking is ideal. Metal can also be used here, as our concern is with the ashes. Any residual tincture in that plant mass is being used to fuel the fire and will be lost. Again, the smoke released from the burning plant residue will be significant; as such, if you do it inside, make sure that the exhaust fan on your stove is functioning.

3. As the feces burns, be sure to turn it with your metal rod. You may gently fan it or blow on it to keep the fire going or to make the coals hotter. However, if you choose to do this, you must take extreme care and should wear protective eyewear.

4. After the salts have cooled, take your pestle and grind them to a fine powder. They will still be black and will contain only a few specks of white or grayish white. Mix in some alcohol until the ashes are slightly damp. Then, ignite the mixture and begin the process again. Do this several times, being sure to grind the powder as fine as possible between each ignition. As you do this, you will notice that the amount of ash is considerably reduced with each incineration.

5. After the third or fourth round, when the amount of lighter ash has increased, take the matter (salt) and place it in a heat-proof dish, covered if possible. Heat it in the oven at 500 or more degrees Fahrenheit until all of it has turned to a gray-white powder or, better still, to a completely white powder. Frequent grinding of the salt even during this phase will assist in this process. (Remember, the finer the particles during the maceration process, the more sulphur extracted; the finer the particles during the calcining process, the easier it is to get the gray-white or white stages of purification.)

6. After the salts have turned as white as you feel is possible, place them in a glass jar that can be tightly sealed while the salts are still warm. This will keep them from absorbing moisture from the air as they cool. Clearly mark the jar with the planetary symbol of the plant if you are working with one plant for each of the planets. If you have more than one herb for a given planet, be sure to mark the name of the plant on the container's label.

If you are eager to test your spagyric product, place a few grains of your tincture's salts in a teaspoon (1 to 2 milliliters, or ten to twenty drops) of the tincture that has been added to a glass of distilled water. This should occur during the planetary hour on the planetary day ruling the herb, in the case of lemon balm, Thursday. If the salts are very pure, they will dissolve, or at least be dramatically reduced, in the tincture and water. Spend a few minutes in a relaxed state after drinking the tincture. You may not feel the effects immediately, but they may arise during periods of meditation or sleep or in other ways across the day. Being familiar with the various areas of life under the influence of each of the planets will help you notice these effects when they take place.

While the salts need not be consumed with the tincture, they will assist in the overall effects of the operation, as they provide the third Essential, or leg, of an alchemical product. It is important to use distilled water, as the energetic traces in spagyric products are pulled toward the salts, or matter, to become "fixed," just as water is absorbed by a sponge. Trace minerals in normal bottled or tap water will draw off a minute amount of the tincture's energy. This is, however, only a small amount and should not prevent anyone from undertaking the experiment.

Once consumed, a feedback loop of energy and increased consciousness is set up within the alchemist's body. This further purifies the material body (salt) of the alchemist, just as the material body (salt) of the plant was purified. With a decrease in blockages, more energy is released within the alchemist's body, making psychic experiments and activities easier to conduct. While the effects of plants are strong, they must be adapted to in stages. Regular consumption of spagyric products is common for students who have yet to begin working with minerals, whose effects are more powerful and longer lasting.

Do not make the mistake of thinking that you could revert to an earlier stage; know only that the energy potential of plants is more limited, and therefore the alchemist using them must fill up his psychic gas tank more often than if he were utilizing mineral products. The distance traveled under their power, however, remains the same.

Above all, remember the sacredness of the operation you have performed. Its intent is regeneration—physically, psychologically, and spiritually—through the assistance of the tincture as a manifestation of your spiritual power. Some alchemists combine this aspect of the work with Qabalistic or astrological invocations, similar to what is done for talismans, to intensify the desired effects.

In the next chapter, we will examine the preparation of the Ens tincture, another simple and highly beneficial experiment. Following that, we will explore the preparation of the Plant Stone.

KEY POINTS

- Alchemy bridges the spiritual and material, uniting them through a manipulation of etheric energies under the direction of the attitude of the alchemist.

- Everything in alchemy is composed of three parts known as essentials or principles, which are: sulphur (soul), mercury (life force), and salt (material matrix).

- The three essentials are composed of the four elements, all of which arise out of the primordial void, known as Chaos or Hyle.

- These three essentials are separated and recombined ("solve et coagula") to perfect their expression.

- The number of cycles of separation and recombining needed to restore harmony between the elements is traditionally seven repetitions.

- Spagyric products are a consumable talisman.

- The fundamental practices of plant and mineral work are the same; only their kingdoms are different.

- Alchemical practices can be seen as having three parts: the Work of the Head, the Work of the Heart, and Work of the the Hands. The Work of the Head is the technical and philosophical material that we must learn and follow. The Work of the Hands is the application of these ideas in the laboratory setting. The Work of the Heart is the synthesis of our experiences in meditation and prayer, which is critical to being a successful alchemist.

GENERAL ASSIGNMENTS FOR CHAPTER TWO

1. Make several drawings for meditation and use in your work area. They should include (1) the three essentials, (2) the Tree of Life, (3) Chaos, and (4) the Philosopher's Stone.

2. Obtain or draw an illustration of Thoth, Hermes, and/or a famous alchemist who inspires you, such as St. Germain, Cagliostro, Paracelsus, Maria the Jewess, or Nicholas Flamel (and his wife, Perenelle), and place them in your work area when studying or performing experiments.

3. Study the chart on planetary hours in Appendix A and calculate the hours for one week.

4. Collect the needed supplies to make a basic tincture for each of the seven ancient planets, as well as sundew for "the planet Earth."

5. Reread this chapter and outline the process for making a tincture in your notebook.

6. Begin each tincture on its planetary day. Note the date, time, planetary hour, and phase of the moon in which you started your experiment. (Sundew can be started on Saturday, during either the first or second planetary hour of Saturn.)

MEDITATION PRACTICES FOR CHAPTER TWO

Just as alchemy has its three essentials of sulphur, mercury, and salt, we can examine the three principal tools used by the aspiring alchemist as having three parts as well. Alchemy is often called a work of the head, heart, and hands. The "head" refers to the ideas that must be learned, memorized, and meditated upon, as well as the instructions that must be followed for each step of the process. Alchemy requires the ability to use reason, formulate possible solutions, and reflect upon what actions have been undertaken and why. The "hands" refers to the actual physical actions taken in a laboratory or in working with raw materials and transforming them into a finished product. The "heart" is the method of meditation, inner listening, and awakened intuition that all students must learn to rely upon if they are to enter into the realm of genuine transformation—that is, the making of superior plant or mineral products that have extraordinary healing powers unexplainable by known laws and the ability to initiate both their creator and others into deeper realms of the soul.

This book is designed to give each student sufficient tools with which to undertake the Work of the Head, Heart, and Hands and thereby become a practicing alchemist. Each chapter contains intellectual study, meditative practices, and practical experiments that are to be carried out so that students who follow these instructions develop their various levels of consciousness in a harmonious manner. Remember, to be a genuine alchemist, you must actually transmute your consciousness and be able to demonstrate its reality to yourself by transmuting something in the material world. While this often makes reference to turning lead into gold, it is sufficient to say that on a lesser level, creating a powerful healing product will also qualify. To paraphrase Paracelsus, "We only transmute without, that which we have first transmuted within."

Meditation is the primary tool for undertaking the Work of the Heart and, in light of Paracelsus's view, is ultimately critical for success in alchemical practices. Traditionally, alchemy would be practiced only after a long period of study in Qabala, astrology, and the fundamentals of Hermeticism. This training would take place either under the direct supervision of a practicing adept or in a lodge setting and would be part of a graded series of initiations and degrees taking place over several years, if not decades. The high point of alchemical lodges came in the eighteenth century, when the German-based Order of the Gold and Rosy Cross was the focal point of European alchemical practices. Several of its documents have survived to the present day, along with a summary of the material covered in its degrees. The Hermetic Order of the Golden Dawn later used the names and titles of these degrees in its Qabalistically based system of initiatic degrees.

To begin the inner phase of alchemical work, it is suggested that you spend ten to twenty minutes a day for ten to fourteen days on each meditation listed below.

MEDITATION: THE BASICS

1. Begin each meditation session by sitting quietly in a chair with your arms relaxed and in your lap or resting on your upper thighs (palms down), taking care to see that your elbows are relaxed and there is no strain on your shoulders or neck. Tuck your chin slightly in to keep your head steady.

2. Inhale deeply through your nose, hold in the breath, and exhale slowly three times. As you do this, feel yourself relax physically, mentally, and emotionally. Notice the increased sense of stability and centeredness as any cares, concerns, or frustrations of the day are swept away with your outgoing breath. There is no set maximum period for this initial relaxation process, and you may do this more than three times if needed in order to achieve the proper mental state before proceeding. Seven and nine repetitions are also very common.

3. Breathe deeply and hold in the breath for a comfortable period of time; then slowly exhale, hold the breath out for a comfortable period of time, and inhale again. Repeat the process for two or three minutes. As you inhale, imagine a brilliant, bluish silver light enter into you through your nose, and imagine that your body is absorbing the energy, starting with your feet and moving up to your head. You can spend as much time on this exercise as you like; however, two to five minutes will be sufficient for our purposes.

4. After you have filled your body with light, imagining in fact that your physical body is being transformed into light through this cyclic breathing, imagine a sphere of brilliant white light about a foot above you. Sense a connection to this light; it is your awareness of your Higher Self or "Angel," from whom

you are seemingly separate. Breathe in, pulling a ray of light from the sphere into your heart, and feel it expand. As the light grows and glows, your sense of separation dissolves, and you sense the inner presence of your Higher Self in the form of compassion, wisdom, and strength.

5. Do this meditation each day for a week, simply sitting in the new state of inner peace that you have learned to create. The entire process should take anywhere from ten to thirty minutes, depending on how much time you would like to spend on it. When done, give thanks for whatever you have experienced, and know that you are growing closer to spiritual wholeness with each practice period.

After a week, you may add an exercise from the following list to your meditation period:

ALCHEMICAL MEDITATIONS
Meditation on Prima Materia

1. Imagine that you are a vast sea of unmanifest potential, like that which Chaos or the Prima Materia represents. This is a dark, heavy, and dynamic energy that begins to stir and move outward from the center, like ripples from a rock thrown in a still pond.

2. Imagine this process of movement suddenly splitting in half, like a cell that divides to create another cell. Feel how this mass of energy, now comprising two connected cells or spheres, seems to pull in two separate directions. From this pull in two seemingly opposite directions, the creation of the poles of energy and matter is accomplished.

3. Spend some time on this part of the meditation. Feel how one side is very dynamic and energetic and the other is still, dense, and stable, and yet the two are connected to each other and inseparable.

4. Imagine now that the active, dynamic sphere begins to pulse again from its center and that this pulsing creates two new spheres within or from the sphere of energy. The sphere or pulse farthest to your right is elemental fire. It is dynamic and explosive. The sphere connected to it is elemental air, or the organizing principle of the universe.

5. Now imagine that the sphere of primal matter also begins to pulse outward and divide into two distinct yet connected fields of energy. The one closest to you is elemental water, or the emotional and liquid aspects of creation. Next to it are the dense, form-creating energies of elemental earth. This is energy at its greatest density. Stay with this basic image as long as you need to, even working with it over several days before moving on to the final stages.

6. Now sense that there are specific and discrete relationships between the various elements that dictate how they combine with each other. These combinations form the three essentials of sulphur, mercury, and salt.

7. Feel fire and air merge with one another—or primal energy (fire) merging with the expansive, directive, and organizing powers of mind (air)—to form sulphur, or self-consciousness.

8. Feel the dense, form-hungry energies of earth combining with the liquid energies of water to form the energetic (etheric) matrix for material life, or salt.

9. Feel the emotional energies of water and the directing energies of air combine to form the link between the two extremes of pure energy (fire) and pure form (earth), or mercury.

Mercury as Spiritus Mundi, or the Astral Light

The purpose of this meditation is to help you attune to the great mass of energy that mercury represents, sometimes called *Spiritus Mundi*, or Spirit of the Earth. Qabalists also refer to it as the astral light, or Great Mediator. Mercury represents both the connective energy of creation and the energy of each domain (plant, mineral, animal) in which it is present. The function of this energy is to unite material bodies, or salt, with consciousness, or sulphur, making mercury the vast connective energy net of creation, as well as the energy itself.

1. Inhale, filling your body with energy, transforming it into a body of light.

2. Allow this body to slowly dissolve into a field of light as you continue inhaling and exhaling a brilliant stream of silver-blue energy.

3. As you inhale and exhale, feel yourself—your consciousness— continue to expand, just as if it were rippling out from the center of a circle, like ripples on a pond.

4. Continue this feeling, imagining that with each exhalation you are reaching deeper into the universal life force or energy, and that with each inhalation you are drawing more energy into your center from the depths of creation. Imagine and feel how this energy unites everything, gives rise to every form, endows it with consciousness, and animates it with life.

5. Continue with this for several minutes.

6. Write down any experiences or insights that may have occurred.

The Alchemical Alembic: "Solve et Coagula"

The vessel in which alchemical operations are undertaken is called an *alembic* and is described as being shaped like a glass egg. This shape allows for the ascent and descent of energies in a slow and natural fashion, and also hints at fertility and rebirth. The shape of the human aura or energy field is also described as being egg-shaped, and this demonstrates the link between outer physical alchemy and inner transcendental alchemy and shows how one is used to support the other. Just after you have undertaken your regular relaxation breathing for meditation and have reached your head, visualize the following:

1. Imagine that you are inside a sphere or egg-shaped vessel of clear crystal or glass.

2. Imagine that you are a point of light, of pure consciousness, inside the vessel and that a mass of dark liquid fills the lower third. Move down and hover over the liquid for a second. Notice the surface move. Move down into the dark waters and descend as deep as possible.

3. As you begin to go deeper, you notice a feeling of warmth increasing. This is the fire that warms the vessel, allowing the process of distillation to take place. Reach the bottom and then ascend back.

4. When you reach the surface of the liquid, continue through the upper two-thirds, straight upward to the top of the vessel.

5. As you reach the top, feel yourself spread out along the glass sides, even as if you were fracturing apart, and slide down back into the water.

6. Feel these individual drops reunite with the whole at the bottom of the vessel, and ascend again as a single point back to the top of the vessel.

7. Continue this process of ascending and descending, separating and recombining, for several minutes.

8. When you are done, imagine that you are a point of consciousness in the center of the egg again. Exit or dissolve the egg, breathe deeply, and return to normal consciousness. Note the different effects this has on your meditation period.

three

CREATING A PLANT STONE

A PLANT STONE: KEY TO THE ASTRAL WORLD

Creating an alchemical or spagyric product is not only simple, it is also among the highest and most reward-ing activities that a student of occult-ism can accomplish. In the creation of

CHAPTER OVERVIEW
- *Plant Stones for Mastering the Astral Worlds*
- *Several Methods of Making a Plant Stone*
- *Sea Salt and Alchemy*

a "Stone," even in the vegetable kingdom, the symbolic balancing of the elements is the basis for its functional reality. With the har-monizing of the plant's sulphur, salt, and mercury, the herb is per-fected in its potential use as a medium of etheric and astral energy. Through its effects on the etheric body and its energy, physical health and wellness can be maintained or restored. A Plant Stone's impact on the astral energies acts upon the subconscious of the alchemist, opening up gateways to expanded levels of consciousness. It is not uncommon, even at this early stage of practice, for many students to report deeper meditative states, increased dreaming, and improved memory upon awakening. Lucid dreaming and astral projection are also possible, thereby demonstrating the subtle but profound poten-tial of these simple herbal products. These experiences also increase aspiring alchemists' confidence in the work they are undertaking and may even energize them to pursue the more complex and dramati-cally rewarding work of mineral alchemy.

There are many ways of making a Vegetable Stone, running from the simple to the complex, and each has its own advantages and drawbacks. For brevity, as well as the increased possibility of success, this chapter will outline several simple methods. Only experience will help decide which method is best for you.

The effects of the Stone, as suggested previously, are both spiritual and material. While physical health may be affected, the primary purpose, at this stage, is to open up a wider range of consciousness to the student. The Stone's effects also represent, in their own fashion, a certain degree of mastery of the "vegetable" nature by the individual who created them. They can be a profound and powerful gateway to the astral realm, and they may take us to the doors of genuine lasting initiation into the archetypal realm (or the animal-Nephesch soul in Qabala). The creation of all seven planetary Stones, and their perfection, represents a physical demonstration of the student's mastery of the Lower Astral (or Yetziric) World in Qabala.

THE ASTRAL WORLD AND ALCHEMY

In Qabala, the universe is often described as having Four Worlds, or four distinct and unique ways of manifesting energy, matter, and consciousness, going from the most subtle manifestation to the most dense. These Four Worlds are often overlaid on the Tree of Life, and in many instances each is given its own complete Tree, making for a total of four Trees. Each Tree represents the often complex relationships between energy, consciousness, and matter that have evolved and shows how they are expressed in Qabalistic philosophy. For our purposes, however, we will describe everything using one Tree of Life and overlay the worlds on top of it. For simple, practical, day-to-day purposes, this will suffice for nearly all of your Qabalistic and alchemical operations.

The world that material life takes place in is the World of Action, or *Assiah*. This includes all material form as well as *part* of the etheric net that gives rise to material form. On the Tree of Life, this is the tenth sphere, known as *Malkuth* in Hebrew. Next is the astral or psychic world, known as the World of Creation, or *Yetzirah*, which is composed of spheres nine through seven. These spheres are *Yesod* (subconscious and instinct), *Hod* (intellect and reason), and *Netzach* (emotions). The World of Formation, or *Briah*, forms the middle part of the Tree and is the world of ideas and archetypal forms. Briah is composed of *Tiphareth* (self and will to act or be), *Geburah* (energy in action), and *Chesed* (mercy and universal love). The first of the worlds to be created, but the final one from our perspective in the material world, is the World of Formation, or *Atziluth*. Atziluth is pure energy and is composed of the most abstract yet concrete of cosmic ideas. The spheres of Atziluth are *Binah* (first form, or cosmic womb), *Hockmah* (first seed, or cosmic impulse to be), and *Kether* (pure being, Unity).

Each sphere has a special and direct influence on spiritual, mental, emotional, and physical life that is expressed through planetary symbols. Kether is Being, so it has no planet to relate to. Hockmah governs the entire zodiac, and Binah is associated with Saturn, the oldest of the traditional seven ancient planets. The remaining spheres and their planets are as follows: Chesed—Jupiter, Geburah—Mars, Tiphareth—Sun, Netzach—Venus, Hod—Mercury, and Yesod—Moon. Malkuth, or Earth, is the recipient of all of the vibrations and influences of each of these spheres, and for that reason, alchemists can find plants and minerals that relate to each of the planets. In some modern schools of Qabala, it is common to give planetary associations to Kether (Uranus) and Hockmah (Neptune), but this is beyond the scope of plant alchemy, as these planets are generational in their astrological influence and we cannot modify them as easily.

In Qabala, these ten levels of the Tree of Life (*Otz Chaim*) are known as *Sephirah* (singular) and *Sephiroth* (plural). These levels are often encountered as spheres, so for simplicity we will refer to them as spheres. Each sphere is a complex relationship of energy, consciousness, and matter, just as each World is. The World of Assiah, or material life, is the only World that is composed of a single sphere—Malkuth. Each of the remaining three Worlds has three spheres, or levels, to it, giving it three very distinct expressions of energy, matter, and consciousness.

In Qabala, each World is assigned an elemental quality. The World of Atziluth is called the World of Fire because its energies are so pure, intense, and dynamic. The World of Briah is called the World of Water because its energies give rise to form. The World of Yetzirah is called the World of Air because it mediates the energies of life and consciousness in both the astral and material worlds. The World of Assiah is called the World of Earth because it is solid, form, and material. In alchemy, however, these worlds are experienced slightly differently, giving rise to a different set of associations. Yetzirah is called the World of Water because of the intense influence its lunar forces have on water, plant life, and material growth; we will also see these lunar forces affect alchemical experiments such as distillation and calcination. Briah, in turn, is referred to as the World of Air because archetypal forms, or mental ideas, give rise before their material counterparts. If you are used to working with the Qabalistic associations, continue to do so in your Qabalistic work, but for alchemy, it is important to adopt the new set of associations.

If you are new to Qabala and find these descriptions of the Four Worlds and all of the cross-connected associations confusing, don't worry. Simply stick to the basic astrological relationships between the herbs, days of the week, and planets, and know that the spiritual goal of plant alchemy is threefold:

1. To utilize the energy bound in the matter of the material world (Assiah) to purify the material body *and* its etheric link to the astral world (Yetzirah).

2. To open up conscious experiences in the astral world that bring emotional and psychic harmony to our being.

3. To assist in bringing mastery over our emotional and psychic nature as expressed through our psychic body—our chief mechanism of spiritual, astral, and psychic connection to the material world and the invisible worlds—and in doing so, prepare us for

inner spiritual initiation. This initiation is the awakening of the Inner Alchemist, or, in magical terms, "Knowledge and Conversation with One's Holy Guardian Angel."

Interestingly enough, experience suggests that an alchemical product of any sort, be it a tincture or a Stone, herbal or mineral, affects the alchemist who created it differently than others who may be exposed to it. The physical healing power appears most dramatically in people who played no role in making the product, whereas the spiritual effects appear strongest in the alchemist who prepared the product. The reason for this could be quite simple. The alchemist is working at a slightly higher vibrational or energetic level than the average person, and certainly higher than one who is physically ill. As a result, the alchemist enjoys better health, fewer illnesses, quicker recovery periods, and the like. The alchemist's energy is increasingly being made more subtle and being directed toward interior experiences and strengthening of the psychic centers. One who is ill, or even not ill but simply not on a spiritual or esoteric path, is operating at a lower level than the alchemist whose vibratory energies have impregnated the tincture or product that he or she has made. When non-alchemists consume the product, they respond to an increased level of physical consciousness, because that is where they focus their attention. This almost always translates into physical or sexual energy of some kind, as energy flows from higher to lower, and for the average person, sex is the lowest common denominator of physical life.

This points out a critical point regarding alchemical privacy and ethics:

1. Hide your stuff so others don't get hurt.

If consumed in bulk, alchemical products, even herbal ones, can be disruptive to the human or animal who ingests them. Besides the obvious alcohol volume involved and its high proof or purity rating, there is also the energetic component. Like homeopathic products, spagyric products should work on the etheric level, and this needs to be respected even if it is not always understood. Keep your finished products out of harm's way by keeping them out of the sight and reach of anyone not directly involved in their creation.

2. Help people whom you know, but do not advertise as an alchemist or practitioner of the spagyric arts.

All states and most countries have rules and regulations regarding the practice of medicine and the prescription of products sold for the purpose of maintaining or restoring health. While you can purchase many herbal, homeopathic, and even spagyric products over the counter or via the Internet, it is best to keep your practice a private concern, even if you are a licensed health care provider. The results achieved from even the simple and easy-to-make spagyric products described in this book are beyond the scope of the average person. If you have results with someone who then cannot be quiet about it, you run the risk of becoming known as a "healer" and having to spend all of your time making products rather than progressing on your path. Then the temptation to create products for sale will enter into the picture, and from this point on, your focus will be no longer alchemy, but commerce. Your path will be derailed before it has even begun. For this very reason, the Order of the Gold and Rosy Cross, the eighteenth-century German alchemical society, forbid its members to have their own laboratories, and instead they worked in common. While one reason for this was the expensive mineral work the members were performing, the society also made the rule to reduce members' temptation to attempt transmutations of base metals into gold in order to maintain their laboratories. Modern technology, glassware, and mineral supplies are considerably cheaper now than in the eighteenth century, so the concern of expense no longer applies, but the moral of the story is still the same. Avoid the temptation of commerce where alchemical and other spiritual matters are concerned. Do not "sell the gifts of God."

3. Don't let anyone handle your products, any more than you would let them handle your magical tools or implements.

Once you have started an experiment, keep prying eyes and hands as far from it as possible. It is best even to keep people and animals out of your laboratory or work area as much as possible, even if this means simply hanging a curtain in front of your space when you are not working. Human energy fields are powerful, both radiating and attracting energy. When a product is being made, that product is very susceptible to energetic influences. It is this very susceptible state that the alchemist seeks to take advantage of when making a product according to planetary influences and, in many instances, lunar and zodiacal influences. However, should a disruptive emotion come near the products, they may potentially be affected. That is why we wrap them in aluminum foil—aluminum kills energetic patterns. The glass insulates the tincture from material disruption, but the foil insulates from psychic disruption. If possible, store your products or works in progress in a cupboard or cabinet that can be locked. In many magical orders, once a student constructs and consecrates his or her magical tools, no one else, not even a superior in the order, is allowed to handle them, for the same reason. The tools are charged talismans with a specific energetic signature created by the combination of their function and the vibratory signature of their creator. The same rule applies to alchemical products.

LUNAR CYCLES AND ALCHEMY

The effect of the Moon and its monthly cycles on dreams, psychic sensitivity, and paranormal phenomena is well known. It is no surprise, then, that the Moon is the most important of the seven ancient planets in the creation of herbal products. Each month, the Moon goes through eight phases, each lasting approximately three and a half days. These phases start with the New Moon, growing in strength (*waxing*) until they reach their apogee with the Full Moon, and then descending (*waning*) toward the next New Moon. The first half of this cycle is considered positive for most works, while the second half is considered negative. By positive, we mean that those operations requiring additional energy are best performed during the waxing period of the moon; those requiring extraction or release are best performed during the waning of the moon. For the practical alchemist, Qabalist, or Witch, knowing which operations to perform and which to avoid during these cycles is critical to success.

The first half of the lunar cycle, or the waxing period, is beneficial for (1) starting alchemical operations; (2) imbibing salt for creating Plant Stones; (3) performing distillation for separating the sulphur from the mercury in a tincture; and (4) enriching of the life force by alchemical or Qabalistic means. The second half of the lunar cycle, or the waning period, is beneficial for (1) distillation of red wine to create alcohol, and (2) purification, such as calcination. These cycles impact additional actions, but these have not been listed because this book does not include their operations.

In this regard, Dion Fortune states:

> It is the light of the Moon which is the stimulative factor in these etheric activities, and as the Earth and Moon share one etheric double, all etheric activities are at their most active when the Moon is at its full. Likewise, during the dark of the Moon, etheric energy is at its lowest, and unorganized forces have a tendency to rise up and give trouble. The Dragon of the Qliphoth [disruptive forces] raises his multiple heads. In consequence, practical occult work is best let alone during the dark by all but experienced workers. The life giving forces are relatively weak and the unbalanced forces relatively strong; the results, in inexperienced hands, is chaos.[1]

While Dion Fortune was a Qabalist and a ritual magician and not a laboratory alchemist, her words are still applicable. A careful study and review of experiments undertaken will demonstrate the close relationship between Qabala, astrology, and alchemy. A quick look at the Tree of Life will show that Mercury and the Moon work together in operations of magic and alchemy. The Moon (Yesod) gives power and connections, whereas Mercury (Hod) gives knowledge

---

1   Dion Fortune, *The Mystical Qabalah* (York Beach, ME: Weiser, 2000), 243.

and skill. Together with the harmonizing and emotionally satisfying influences of Venus (Netzach), these three planets open up the inner worlds and bring the alchemist closer to inner awakening.

In addition to its eight cycles and two principal phases of waxing and waning, the Moon also experiences a "mini-year" each month as each of the signs of the zodiac pass under her influence. These zodiacal periods last about two and a quarter days each and can be used in conjunction with planetary hours, as well as the waxing and waning phases, to further increase the astral influence in the creation of an alchemical product. Utilizing these cycles to their fullest benefit is the foundation of Renaissance natural magic and should be done by every aspiring student of the art. However, the ability to maximize these two cycles does not happen every month, and some advance planning is necessary if you wish to compound these energies.

The Moon is in the same sign as the Sun during the New Moon, and it moves one sign approximately every two and a quarter days. Thus, if the Moon is in Aries and the Sun is in Aries, then nine days later the Moon will be four signs ahead, or in Cancer. This is a very rough way to estimate the position of the Moon in relation to the zodiac. Referencing an inexpensive astrological program, online source, or either Llewellyn's *Moon Sign Book* or *Wicca Almanac* is preferred.

For example, if you were to create an herbal tincture of Mercury to assist in interior work, then it would be preferable to undertake this operation on a Wednesday morning during a New Moon, with the Sun in Gemini or Virgo. If, however, it were not possible to wait until those signs came around, then an operation when the Moon is waxing *and* in Gemini or Virgo could substitute.

HOW TO MAKE A PLANT STONE

The process of making a Vegetable Stone is similar to that of making a spagyric tincture, as previously described. However, instead of having the option of disposing of the plant residue, or salt, you must calcine it and keep it for future use in order to make a Plant Stone. If the salt you obtained from the plant matter is insufficient in volume because you did not use a large amount of herb, you may substitute sea salt. In the event that you need more salt, you can burn dry herb of the same plant used to make the tincture, reduce its ashes to a fine gray-white or white powder, and add them to the salt of the original tincture. However, be clear on this: if the tincture is lemon balm and there is insufficient salt after calcining the plant residue to begin working on a Stone, then you can reduce more lemon balm to an ash without having to make it into a tincture first, because it is the ash, or salt, you want, and not the sulphur. You should not substitute other plants, as they will differ in their planetary signatures, thereby affecting the outcome of the experiment.

LEACHING SALTS

Leaching of the salt may also yield up greater progress in the final stages of balancing the elements.

Equipment Needed

- Smooth, flat-bottomed glass or Pyrex baking dish.
- Several ounces of distilled water. Distilled water can be purchased from a grocery or drug store.
- Desk lamp or toaster oven.
- Butterknife, spatula, or other instrument to scrape the salts off the surface of the baking dish.
- Salts calcined to a gray-white color.
- Container for the salts.

Leaching is accomplished by placing the salt in a thin layer on the surface of a glass or Pyrex baking dish. A moderate amount of distilled water is then added and evaporated naturally or with the assistance of a heat lamp or toaster oven. The salt is then scraped off the container, ground, and recalcined. Experience has shown that leaching can be done in fifteen to thirty minutes if the salt is finely spread and the heat source is close by. A simple desk lamp, with as low as a 7½-watt bulb, will be sufficient.

The sulphur and mercury, which have previously been together in the tincture, in some instances are separated into their respective aspects. Thus, in the creation of a Stone, we have three separate materials that we will recombine in the alchemical laboratory.

If separation of the sulphur from the mercury—or essential oils from the alcohol—is not possible because of equipment limitations, then they may be used together, but this may affect the quality of the Stone produced. An "artificial" Plant Stone may also be made with sea salt, alcohol, and high-grade essential oils of the desired plant. Above all, it is important to note that a Vegetable Stone takes time to produce—in some cases up to several months—and will change in color and texture after it is created. Patience, dedication, and confidence are the needed attributes at this stage.

Method I

Preparation is the key to success in alchemical work. Preparation of the materials, of the place of working, and above all, of the attitude of the worker are needed. The attitude must be a mixture of humility and unswerving confidence in the ultimate success of the undertaking. An internal image and a feeling of the product coming into being, up to the final moment it is realized, will greatly assist in its creation. Meditate and visualize the successful completion of the work often.

Remember the words of Heinrich Khunrath, "Ora et labora," or "Prayer and work," and the aphorism on the fourteenth plate of the *Mutus Liber*, "Ora, lege, lege, lege, relege, labora et invenies," or "Pray, read, read, read, reread, work, and [you will] discover [it]." Note the order of the directions: prayer comes first, then reading and rereading, and finally the material operations.

While alchemists work alone, or at best with a mate, they do the work not for themselves only, but to assist in the relieving of pain and suffering of others. Their motive is well expressed in the motto of the Knights Templar, which comes from the 115th Psalm and which they sang in victory: "Non nobis Domine! Non nobis, sed nomini tuo da Gloriam." That is, "Not unto us, O Lord! Not unto us, but unto Thy name give Glory." This is ever the motto of a true alchemist.

THE STONE

You may calcine the salt ahead of time, or you may wait until the planetary hour on the day of the ruling planet of the herb. Some alchemists find that in preparation of the salts, placing a small, fine wire mesh screen over the dish used for calcining will help hold the ashes down. This is important, as the finer, lighter ash will easily blow away, and it is this fine white ash that is important for the creation of a Vegetable Stone. A slow but safe alternative is to place small amounts of the ash in a crucible and to allow the heat from your gas stove to envelop the crucible. You will need tongs, as the crucible will grow very hot.

Equipment Needed
- Plant salts finely ground and calcined to a pure white or near-white color.
- Plant tincture extracted from the plant whose salts are used in the creation of the Plant Stone.
- Clean eyedropper.
- Small ceramic crucible and lid.
- Crucible tongs.
- Heat source, such as a gas stovetop or a small, hand-held blowtorch.
- Wire triangle, preferably with ceramic insulation, to hold the crucible in place as it is heated. This can easily be made from three pieces of thick metal wire (such as that of a coat hanger) twisted at the ends and pressed in at the sides to hold the crucible steady.

- Small container for the newly created Plant Stone to be placed in when completed.

- Patience, patience, and more patience.

The Process

1. Carefully read all directions several times prior to undertaking the experiment. Be sure you know every step of the way. Remember: Safety first!

2. If the salt is white or near-white, place it in a heat-resistant dish or crucible on a low heat source. The heat may be modulated, but under no circumstances let it burn or scorch the herb.

3. Slowly, drop by drop, begin to place the tincture into the heated salt until it is completely absorbed. This is called *imbibition*, or imbibing the Stone with life (mercury) and soul (sulphur). You are, in essence, reincarnating the vegetable power of the plant.

4. Continue this process for as long as you like, or stop after one full hour, either planetary or secular.

5. Begin again either next week or on another day, preferably Saturday, on the planetary hour of the plant. If this is inconvenient, then begin at any hour when the work can be done.

6. Between the phases of imbibition, keep the Stone in a place away from prying eyes and, if possible, sunlight. (Whether it be in the womb or under the earth, many good things like to grow in the dark.)

7. When the Stone will accept no more liquid, place it where you can observe the changes that may take place over the next few months.

8. If possible, store the Stone near a heat source, such as in an incubator or near a gas oven range with a running pilot light, if one is available.

9. If the Stone suddenly jells, quickly pour it out of the crucible into a thimble, as it will harden and be difficult to get out of the porcelain crucible. This hardening is desirable, compared with the softer, easily consumable Stones that may appear.

If the Stone is soft like licorice, then it may be ingested in small slivers under the tongue or with a glass of distilled water. If the Stone is hard, then place it in a glass of distilled water for several minutes so that it may transfer its power to the water, and then drink the water.

If the Stone is perfected, repeated immersion will not degrade or "attack" the Stone. Otherwise, expect it to dissolve over time. It is imperative that you keep a careful record of the days, times, and phases of the Moon during which the work is done. It is strongly urged that work not be done during the "dark phase" of the Moon. New Moon and Full Moon periods are most beneficial, as with most psychic activities or projects.

Method II

A low-tech way to make a Stone without the use of open flame is to use an incubator while imbibing the salts over a period of six months to one year. All that you need is a 10- or 15-watt bulb placed inside of a Styrofoam cooler or box. The socket and extension cord can be unscrewed from a standard work light found in a hardware store. These inexpensive lights have silver dishes to reflect the light and clips that allow them to be hung in a variety of locations. Simply cut a hole in the side of the Styrofoam cooler, insert the socket through the hole, attach a "washer" cut from corrugated cardboard to help hold it in place, and you are done. You can also place a brick inside the incubator to hold it in place as well as to hold in heat. Place your crucible on top of the brick and imbibe the salts during the planetary hour of its ruling planet and day. For example, if the herb used is lemon balm, the salts would have to be imbibed only once a week, during the planetary hour of Jupiter on Thursday. Of course, you could imbibe the Stone on additional planetary hours of Jupiter to speed up the process, but this is not required.

SEA SALT AND ALCHEMY

If salts from the plant used to make the tincture are not available, an "artificial" Stone may be made in its place using a similar process. In place of the calcined residue, sea salt is soaked in rainwater and dried several times, being crushed with mortar and pestle between cycles. The aura and energy radiating from the hands of the alchemist are most crucial in the work. That is why during the handling of the salt and tincture, the attitude of the alchemist is so important; it is also why alchemists work alone, undisturbed by the inquisitive and disruptive thoughts of others.

While it should not have to be said to someone interested in alchemical, Qabalistic, or Hermetic work, we will state it again to drive the point home: thoughts are real things on their way to becoming tangible in our material world. It is for this reason that we mentally wrap ourselves in a blanket or veil to psychically isolate ourselves from the disruptive psychic energy of others, and why we wrap our products in aluminum foil when they are completed. Alcohol is very susceptible to psychic vibrations, as is cold water, and both act as storage mediums for those concentrated energies. Consider this the next time you are in a bar or drinking an alcoholic beverage. In Alcoholics Anonymous, it is said that the recovering addict must avoid "stinking thinking," as that is what drives them back to drinking and drugging. When you consider that many alcoholics sit and stew over what is bothering them while clutching an ice-cold drink between their hands, deep in an inner contemplation of failure, anger, and self-destruction, and then consume their "desecrated talismans" one after the other, is it any surprise that alcohol and drug abuse is so destructive to the body and soul of individuals and society?

Equipment Needed

In addition to the equipment listed above, the following will be needed:

- French or Celtic sea salt.
- Additional essential oils, commercially produced, matching the herb being used (may be needed).

If you chose not to soak the sea salt, then crush it, imagining that, like the plant salt, it is opening itself up to the creative powers of the tincture, or cosmic energy and consciousness.

On the appropriate planetary day and hour, begin the imbibing process with an eyedropper, first with grain alcohol until saturated, and then with essential oil. Repeat several times, and proceed as discussed in the previous method.

Modern salt-refining techniques are indebted to the ancient alchemists for much of their methods. The sea and its symbols have been a rich inspiration for alchemists and mystics of all periods. It is not surprising, then, to learn that the ocean itself, the very source from which our physical bodies have arisen, is also the source of much of our foodstuffs as well as potential medicines. The salty waters of *Eaux-Meres*, or "Mother Waters," is the basis of our plasma, amniotic water, and all of our body fluids. For this reason, *only* sea salt that is naturally refined and collected (i.e., organic) is suitable for this work. Salt mined from deep inland or strip-mined off the beaches is "alchemically polluted" and will not do for this work of rejuvenation. Salt produced in the slow, natural manner contains over eighty-four trace minerals, many of which are absent from produced salts, and is gray-brown in color.

Making a Plant Stone from Sea Salt

To make an artificial Plant Stone from sea salt, perform all of the steps in Method I or Method II, and in place of plant salts use organic sea salt. Be sure to dry the salt under a lamp or in an oven at a low temperature before using it, as salt will absorb moisture from the air unless stored in an airtight container. Moisture in the salt will delay the process as well as inhibit the absorption of the sulphur and mercury. Take a few extra minutes to prepare your sea salt accordingly.

SUGGESTIONS FOR STUDY

Before engaging in any of the experiments outlined here, read and reread the material several times, keeping your notebook nearby. Outline the steps in each technique. When performing the experiments, pay attention to your notes and write down each step as you take it. Compare your working list with the master list in your notebook. This may seem trivial, but this regime will give you the habit of noting what you do as you do it. If you decide to do more complex experiments, you will have already formed the required safety and notation habits necessary for the work. As stated earlier, most plant work is relatively safe; if you mislabel something, you can throw it out or test it under your tongue. Metallic work is much less forgiving. Good habits formed early last a lifetime. Not to mention, they save a lot of work later!

KEY POINTS

- Plant Stones represent a higher mastery of the etheric and astral energies than do simple tinctures.
- Plant Stones have several levels of completion, from those that dissolve with use over time to hard pebbles that retain their form after extensive use.
- Moon cycles exert significant influences over the various phases of the work, particularly spagyrics.
- Organic sea salt may be used as a substitute for calcined plant salts.
- Alcohol is susceptible to psychic vibrations, particularly when cold or in a vapor state.

- Our attitude when working must be positive, confident, generous, and focused on the end goal or purpose of the experiment.

- "Ora, lege, lege, lege, relege, labora et invenies," or "Pray, read, read, read, reread, work, and [you will] discover [it]," is an important alchemical motto.

GENERAL ASSIGNMENTS FOR CHAPTER THREE

1. Undertake the creation of a Plant Stone using each of the methods described.

2. Using a calendar, the *Farmer's Almanac*, or Llewellyn's *Moon Sign Book* or *Wicca Almanac*, identify the Full Moon and New Moon periods.

3. Using the above almanacs or other astrological sources, locate the Moon and what sign of the zodiac it is in currently. Locate several optimal times for creating tinctures and working on Plant Stones based on the information in this chapter.

MEDITATION PRACTICES FOR CHAPTER THREE

Lunar Meditation

Perform the following meditation facing the waxing and Full Moon as often as possible, and preferably in or near your garden or the plants that you use for your spagyric work.

1. Imagine that the rays of the moon are penetrating you and that you are being transformed into a "lunar" being.

2. Imagine or sense the etheric or subtle energy of Earth and its intimate connection to the Moon and its influences. The etheric energy can be imagined as bluish gray with flecks of silver interpenetrating everything around and inside of you.

3. Do this for ten to twenty minutes at night.

4. Note any impression in your journal, and pay attention to your dreams and psychic impressions.

Spagyric Operations

Visualizing the entire operation of making a Plant Stone from beginning to end in perfect detail dramatically assists in making better products. Do this several times with each herb for each planet you are working with. Pay attention to whatever insights you may have about the process.

1. Review your outline of the spagyric process, from making a tincture and calcining the herb to making a Plant Stone. Visualize the entire process being perfectly executed. Add as much detail as you can from memory.

2. Include the parts of the process you do not directly see, such as the creation of the tincture in the foil-wrapped jar.

3. Imagine the effects of the Moon on the various phases of your work.

4. Contemplate your reasons for creating this alchemical product, and think about the success that you will have when it is completed.

5. Do this several times, and note your response to the various phases.

The Great Mother

Meditate on the nature of the sea and how all life as we know it came from it. Do some research on the sea and sea salt, and devise your own meditations based on the mythological and scientific information you discover. Note the importance of lunar cycles on ocean tides.

four

DISTILLATION

The methods previously outlined for creating a Plant Stone will be useful for situations in which time or tools are limited, as well as providing a quick introduction to the operations of alchemy. However, alchemy is like all ar-

eas of meaningful study: the more time, energy, and attention you put into it, the more you will get out of it. What we get out of alchemy are the means to heal ourselves and others and assist in the reintegration of Nature into our daily lives. Each of us must decide how important that is to us, and act accordingly.

To better understand the alchemical maxim "solve et coagula," it is important to undertake the process of distillation. *Distillation* is the heating of liquids or solids, condensing the vapor given off, and then cooling the liquid retrieved so that it is purified. In spagyric operations, our primary use for distillation is (1) to create highly pure alcohol from red wine for use as a menstruum for the creation of herbal tinctures and (2) to separate the principal components of a tincture, or the mercury from the sulphur.

Distillation of herbal products is done at very low temperatures and can be carried out with a few simple tools. Laboratory glassware to perform a simple distillation can be obtained easily and inexpensively and speeds up the process by making it more efficient. Otherwise, the procedure described here is the same, as it is based on the same principles: a liquid is heated, the steam or vapor let off is collected and cooled, and the liquid is retrieved.

In alchemy, the process of separating and recombining allows for a liquid pulled from a tincture to grow stronger (more pure) with each successive round of distillation. As the alcohol is pulled from wine, the process allows the alcohol to be used as a menstruum without bringing in the additional components that make wine. For mercury that is pulled from a tincture and remixed with the sulphur, the mercury is able to make the sulphur (or essential oils, fats, and so on) of the plant more subtle and penetrating in its operations.

RED WINE AND ALCHEMY

Alcohol is created by the *fermentation*, or decomposition, of plant matter. As it decays, chemical reactions occur that transform the water released into alcohol. Each type of alcohol made in this fashion, either commercially or by Nature, will have an odor and flavor distinct from the signature of the plant or plants it is derived from. This signature in some ways acts as a minor homeopathic tincturing to the herbal or spagyric product being created. It is impossible to completely eradicate this organic mark, and some alchemists see this as an impurity in their work. These alchemists claim that the only true spagyric product is one that is fermented in its own alcohol, thereby creating its own mercury with its own unique signature, and is completely pure in its part. A tincture like this is made in the same fashion that wine or beer is brewed.

While this is open to debate, both products created by fermentation and the addition of alcohol from an outside source produce strange and wonderful effects. However, one thing that is strongly encouraged is that each alchemist create his or her own "philosophic" mercury for use in spagyric products through the distillation of alcohol from red wine. According to the doctrines of sympathetic and natural magic, only red wine will do. The quality of the wine is unimportant; it only needs to have a high enough alcohol yield to be worth the effort. Wine averages between 8 and 12 percent alcohol by volume. This means that with an average alcohol volume of 10 percent, a gallon of red wine will yield approximately 6.4 ounces of alcohol. Fortunately, the cheaper wines often sold in gallon bottles have a higher alcohol yield, averaging 12 percent and even approaching 20 percent. This means that with the right red wine, slightly over 12.5 ounces of alcohol can be recovered.

It is important to note that the wine must be made exclusively from red grapes and must not be a fruit wine or have other flavoring additives. Red wine is exceptionally useful because of its signature rather than in spite of it. Wine is made from pressing and fermenting whole red grapes. It is well known that "red fruits" are exceedingly beneficial to the body and high in *antioxidants*, substances that prevent free radicals from going about their business, which in humans is facilitating the aging process. The skin of red grapes contains the highest yield of antioxidants. For this reason, drinking red grape juice is as beneficial as drinking red wine. Red grapes are considered solar in nature, or having a powerful relationship to the Sun, and they have the ability to convey its life-giving energies more directly than a non-solar plant. The symbolic relationship between red wine and the energies of life is well known in rituals, particularly that of the Christian Mass. Alchemists who spend the time preparing their own plant mercury from red wine will benefit greatly and will see the subtle difference in their finished products.

DISTILLING ALCOHOL FROM RED WINE
Equipment Needed for a Simple Distillation
- Large flask—500 milliliters or larger.
- Receiving flask—no less than 250 milliliters, preferably 500 milliliters.
- Rubber or waxed cork stoppers for flasks.
- Three feet of silicon rubber tubing *or* glass tube.
- Two pieces of glass tubing, each approximately one inch long.
- Container for cold water, no less than two inches deep.

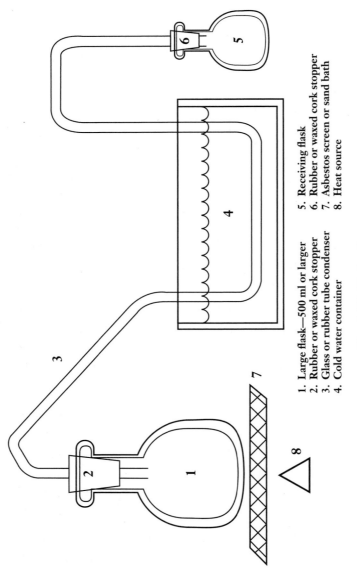

1. Large flask—500 ml or larger
2. Rubber or waxed cork stopper
3. Glass or rubber tube condenser
4. Cold water container

5. Receiving flask
6. Rubber or waxed cork stopper
7. Asbestos screen or sand bath
8. Heat source

Simple Distillation Setup

- Asbestos screen or sand bath.

- Heat source, such as a kitchen stove.

- Water source and/or ice.

- Large siphon or turkey baster to remove water from container as it warms.

How to Distill

Distillation is a very simple and easy process. It is, however, time consuming, depending on the volume of fluid you are working with. To assist in your understanding of the process involved, keep the diagram of the distillation setup in front of you as you read these instructions, and take the time to copy it into your notebook.

Safety Precautions

- Remember: Safety first! Make sure your work area is stable and will not be disturbed while in use.

- Alcohol burns at a low temperature and is easily extinguished by smothering with baking soda or a large wet towel. Keep one or both of these handy in case of an accident, and above all, don't panic. Every alchemist has at least one explosion at some point in his or her laboratory career, and you will most likely have one as well.

- Do not leave your distillation unattended when it is running.

- Work alone. Make sure your space is free from animals, children, and prying eyes, and turn off other disturbances such as telephones and pagers.

The Technique

1. Read all directions several times prior to undertaking the experiment. Be sure that you clearly understand each step. Remember: Safety first!

2. Fill the large flask about one-third of the way with several ounces of red wine. You may want to measure the amount of

wine first so that you can get a rough estimate of how much will be distilled off as the process begins.

3. Connect both ends of the rubber tubing to the small pieces of glass tubing.

4. Insert both ends of the tubing into the rubber or cork stopper. The stoppers may have holes already drilled in them, or you may have to make the holes yourself with a hand drill.

5. Stopper the large flask containing the red wine.

6. Stopper the receiving flask.

7. Place an asbestos screen on your gas range, and put your large flask on top of it. If you do not have an asbestos screen, you can use a small Pyrex or terra cotta plate filled with clean sand instead. After repeated use, the terra cotta will weaken and break, so watch for cracks. The sand absorbs and distributes the heat so that the flask does not take a direct flame; it also allows for an even distribution of a gentler heat across the bottom surface of the liquid.

8. Place your receiving flask in a secure position opposite the large flask, and immerse the rubber tubing in the water basin. The water should be cold, or at least cool. You can add ice if needed, and non-melting ice packs can also be used.

9. Turn the heat on beneath your large flask. After several minutes, you may see a white vapor in the upper part of the flask. If the liquid should start to form small bubbles on the surface, it has begun to boil and the heat must be turned back immediately.

10. Check your receiving flask to see if any distillate has been collected. If you do not see drops of liquid falling into it, shake it gently to see if any have been collected, as they can be so clear that they may be initially missed until sufficient volume is built up.

11. Continue this until you have collected an amount of fluid slightly less than you have estimated as the amount you expect to recoup.

12. Alcohol boils at a lower temperature than water; thus, the surface of the liquid should not be allowed to boil, as this means water is going over with the alcohol.

13. After you have collected your alcohol, allow your equipment to cool. Clean it with strong soap and water and let it dry.

14. Repeat this operation until you have 4 to 8 ounces, or enough alcohol to make a tincture.

15. Once you have collected your alcohol, place it in the large flask and purify it by distilling it six more times, for a total of seven distillations.

Removing the Remaining Water

It is impossible to make absolutely pure alcohol using this method. While the product will be very pure, possibly 90 percent (180 proof) or better, there is an additional operation that you will undertake to decrease the amount of water mixed with the alcohol, thereby sharpening it.

1. Place your alcohol in a jar or flask that can be tightly sealed.

2. Grind several grams of potassium carbonate and place it on a cookie sheet or pie tin in the oven for several minutes to dry out.

3. Once it is dry, open the vessel containing your alcohol and quickly pour it in, using a funnel. Avoid making contact with the powder or breathing it, as it is caustic.

4. Seal the vessel tightly and let it sit overnight.

5. Distill off the alcohol.

The process of repeated distillation is critical in the making of alcohol used in spagyric products. As the vapor rises, it is highly susceptible to psychic influence and is highly charged by the environment, the attitude of the alchemist, and the astral influences of the planetary hours. Repeated separation and recombination creates a menstruum that is very sharp or acute, that is, capable of penetrating the herb and extracting its sulphur. The benefits derived from this additional work will only be obvious to an experienced alchemist, someone who has realized the healing and spiritualizing value of the simple experiments given earlier and seeks to enhance them.

The process of distillation works the same regardless of which tools you choose to use. The laboratory glassware listed below will make the process easier and faster but will not alter the process. This brings up an important point: when examining old alchemical manuscripts and engravings, seek to understand the function of the tools, and then you will understand the process. In distillation, the function of a rubber tube or glass fractionating column is the same: to provide a surface for vapor to come into contact with a cooling agent (water or ice) so that it can condense into liquid. Prior to the widespread use of distillation equipment, or in the absence of running water, alchemists used a device known as a retort. A *retort* is a round-bottomed flask that has an opening in the top, which is closed with a glass stopper when in use, and has a long glass tube or neck running off the top at a downward angle. The length of the attached glass tube acts in the same manner as the rubber tubing or cooling column, only instead of water, air temperature is used, which produces a slower cooling cycle.

Equipment for a Simple Laboratory Distillation Train

- Large flask—500 milliliters or larger.
- Receiving flask—no less than 250 milliliters, preferably 500 milliliters.
- Fractionating column (glass).
- Thermometer.

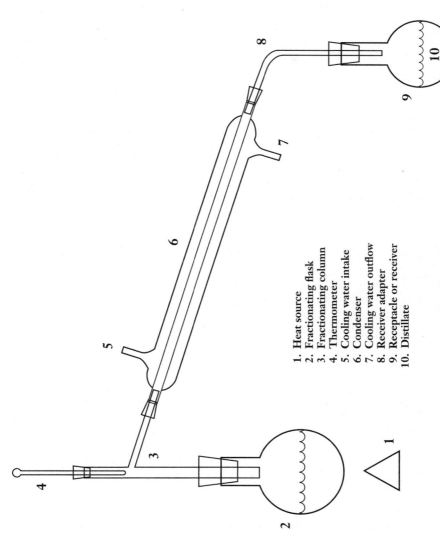

1. Heat source
2. Fractionating flask
3. Fractionating column
4. Thermometer
5. Cooling water intake
6. Condenser
7. Cooling water outflow
8. Receiver adapter
9. Receptacle or receiver
10. Distillate

Distillation Train

- Condenser (glass).
- Receiver adapter.
- Heat source.
- Water source.
- Two metal stands and clips to hold glassware in place when in use.

You can obtain the above laboratory setup new or used inexpensively from several reputable supply houses, as well as from Internet sources such as eBay and LabEx, with costs ranging from $75 to $150. You must exercise caution in purchasing used equipment, as toxic residue may be present and may contaminate your products, making them unusable. If you purchase secondhand equipment, be absolutely positive how it was used and cleaned prior to sale and shipment.

DISTILLATION AND CREATING A PLANT STONE

Just as distillation can be used to produce a highly purified and psychically enriched menstruum from red wine, it can also be used to strengthen and refine existing tinctures, create Elixirs, and produce higher-quality Plant Stones.

Strengthening a Tincture: Method I

1. Place your tincture in the large flask.
2. Place pure white calcined salts in the receiving flask.
3. Distill mercury over into the receiving flask.
4. Filter the salts with fine-grade filter paper and dry them.
5. Grind salts to a powder and place back into the receiving flask.
6. Return mercury to the large flask, mix with sulphur, and repeat the process six more times.

When working with your tincture in this manner, you must be very careful not to scorch or burn your sulphur. It will thicken and turn into a syrup, often called "honey" in alchemical texts, but it must not be allowed to overheat, or it will be ruined.

Method II

Method II is identical to Method I, only the salts are not used to filter the mercury. The mercury is distilled off the sulphur seven times, and with the final distillation it is kept separate. These two essentials will then be added to the salt in the same manner as previously described to create a Plant Stone.

Creating a Plant Stone with the Three Essentials

1. If the salt is white or near-white, place it in a heat-resistant dish or crucible on a heat source turned low. The heat may be modulated, but under no circumstances let it burn or scorch the herb.

2. Slowly, drop by drop, place the mercury and sulphur into the heated salt until they are completely absorbed. This is called *imbibition*, or imbibing the Stone with life (mercury) and soul (sulphur). You are, in essence, reincarnating the vegetable power of the plant. However, unlike your previous experiment, you are recombining all three essentials in their separate forms.

3. Continue this process for as long as you like, or stop after one full hour, either planetary or secular.

4. Begin again either next week or on another day, preferably Saturday, on the planetary hour of the plant. If this is inconvenient, then begin at any hour when the work can be done.

5. Between the phases of imbibition, keep the Stone in a place away from prying eyes and, if possible, sunlight. Remember, whether it be in the womb or under the earth, many good things like to grow in the dark.

6. When the Stone will accept no more liquid, place it where you can observe the changes that may take place over the next few months.

7. If possible, store the Stone near a heat source, such as in an incubator or near a gas oven range with a running pilot light, if one is available.

8. If the Stone suddenly jells, quickly pour it out of the crucible into a thimble, as it will harden and be difficult to get out of the porcelain crucible. This hardening is desirable, compared with the softer, easily consumable Stones that may appear.

CREATING AN ELIXIR

An *Elixir* is a highly refined tincture or combination of tinctures in a single product. This ability to combine several spagyric products into one medicine allows for the maximum strengthening of their qualities. Here are several possible combinations based on Qabalistic and astrological affinities. A careful study of the planets and their attributes will reveal additional areas of influence.

Moon—Tinctures or Elixirs from lunar plants are beneficial to working with the subconscious, hypnotism, etheric energies, lucid dreaming, astral projection, strengthening of the aura, and the neutralizing of negative karma through action on the psychic level of Yesod, eliminating the possibility of their physical manifestation.

Mercury—Tinctures or Elixirs made from Mercurial plants enhance the mind and communication on all levels, between people and within us. Alchemical and Qabalistic work benefits, as does all magical work involving ritual and the creation of forms and patterns, along with chanting, singing, writing, and strengthening the impact of our thoughts on the astral realm. Mercury offers initiation into the inner temple.

Venus—Tinctures or Elixirs made from plants ruled by Venus are beneficial to our social interaction with others and cultural, artistic, and sexual refinement. Harmonizing of inner energies, including the seven major psychic centers, is done through Venus, and a direct inner contact with Nature's hidden powers, particularly in plants, can be experienced.

Sun—Tinctures and Elixirs made from solar plants strengthen our sense of self, assist us in understanding our relation to others in the cosmic scheme of things, and bring self-confidence, to the point of pride even, so that we can undertake the Great Work. Solar tinctures enhance an awakening of the Inner Alchemist, or "Knowledge and Conversation with One's Holy Guardian Angel."

Mars—Tinctures and Elixirs of plants ruled by Mars strengthen the physical and psychic bodies, particularly on the level of reflex and instinct. Sexual and survival drives are enhanced, blood purified, and muscle tone increased. Mars also enhances the projection of psychic power.

Jupiter—Tinctures and Elixirs of plants ruled by Jupiter are beneficial to general health and well-being. They provide insight into religion, law, philosophy, wealth, rituals, and ceremonies of all kinds. Jupiter bestows Divine Mercy and compassion, and provides for an awakening of the divine name of the Tetragrammaton.

Saturn—Tinctures and Elixirs of plants ruled by Saturn strengthen structures, the bones, teeth, and material supports. They provide patience as well as an understanding of the concepts of time and eternity in relation to our spiritual path. The law of cause and effect is understood through Saturn, and power to bring about manifestation in the material world is enhanced.

If we take the above information and use basic occult principles, we can quickly determine the effects of the following combinations:

Sun and **Mars** enhances strength and ego.

Sun and **Jupiter** opens the highest pathways of cosmic realization.

Sun and **Saturn** reveals the destiny of Self, both spiritual and earthly.

Sun and **Mercury** gives insights into magic and alchemy and provides personal Illumination.

Moon and **Saturn** gives profound psychic sensitivity to material life and psychic forces of karma.

Moon and **Sun** offers a balancing of inner and outer self, the alchemical marriage to a degree.

Moon and **Venus** provides a special understanding of human emotions and astral influences in biological affairs of plants, humans, and animals.

Mercury and **Mars** offers speed and power to thoughts, enhancing psychic phenomena.

Mercury and **Saturn** is the key to hidden occult mysteries.

Mercury and **Venus** offers a harmonizing of intellect and emotions in the personality.

Jupiter and **Venus** opens the energies of expansion and mercy into human relations.

Jupiter, Mars, and **Sun** strengthens self-awareness of the soul.

Mercury, Venus, and **Moon** strengthens the energies of the psychic body and its projection.

Saturn, Sun, and **Moon** strengthens the entire spectrum of consciousness.

KEY POINTS

- Distillation is used to separate liquids and purify them.

- Alcohol distilled from red wine is the preferred source of alcohol for spagyric tinctures.

- Distillation can be done either with simple rubber tubing and several flasks or with laboratory glassware.

- Distillation allows for a product to become rarified in its subtle energy through the principle of "solve et coagula."

- Tinctures can be distilled to separate the mercury from the sulphur.

- The separated mercury and sulphur can be used to create stronger tinctures or a Plant Stone.

- Distillation can be used to create combinations of tinctures known as Elixirs. By combining tinctures together, their subtle, planetary, or astral influences can be mixed in a harmonious manner.

- Specific Elixirs are recommended for aspiring alchemists to assist them in accessing higher knowledge, decreasing the influences of negative karmic traces, and gaining greater mastery over their inner world.

GENERAL ASSIGNMENTS FOR CHAPTER FOUR

- Distill 6 ounces of alcohol from red wine and create a tincture with it.

- Distill a tincture that you have made. Compare its effects after four distillations to those of the initial product. Compare the effects again after seven distillations.

- Make a Plant Stone or an Elixir from the list of possible combinations.

MEDITATION PRACTICES FOR CHAPTER FOUR

Distillation Process in Nature

After preparing yourself for meditation, continue with the following:

1. Imagine that you are sitting in a cave in a warm climate and that it starts to rain.

2. Visualize that you are among the clouds, with their vapors and lightning flashes.

3. Feel the vapor condense and raindrops form. Feel the electricity in the air permeate the clouds and feel rain as it forms and begins to fall.

4. Feel the energized rain hit the earth and descend into the earth, giving its energy to the plants and other organisms.

5. Imagine now that the sun is shining. Feel the heat of the sun dry the earth, even penetrate it, drawing out the water that had seeped down into the soil.

6. Feel the water warm and turn into vapor, a mist of fog covering the early-morning grass.

7. Imagine the heat increase with the onset of day. Imagine the vapor rise and return to the clouds and mingle with them.

Meditation on an Elixir

1. Form a strong emotional concept of what you seek to accomplish by creating an Elixir. Identify the qualities that the plant or plants bring to the realization of that goal.

2. Visualize yourself already having the qualities desired or already having achieved the goal.

3. Notice your emotional reaction to it. Is it overwhelmingly positive? Is there a hint of fear or trepidation? What does success mean?

4. Imagine yourself in the retort; the vaporization or the liquid becomes the subtle etherealization of your inner energies. Feel

the energies free themselves from the attraction to matter and become strong, vibrant, and emotionally charged.

5. As they descend back into the dark liquid of the tincture, feel the tincture become more vibrant and light, ready to release its energies.

6. Continue with this meditation for several minutes; record your results when you are finished.

five

WATER DISTILLATION

Water is a key element in alchemy, both metaphysically when we speak of the elements and as an essential tool of the work. The primary power of water is in assisting the creation of forms for the expression of consciousness, providing nutrition for their continued existence,

and physical purification. Water achieves the first two goals by acting as a conduit for higher, more intense psychic energy. We stated earlier that energy can only be transferred from one body to another in a liquid state: blood transfers physical and psychic nutrition to the organs of the body; endocrine secretions transfer specialized "orders" for the body's health and well-being; and sexual fluids transfer the very essence of life.

This fundamental idea of energy transfer through liquids applies to vapor as well. It is in vapor form that liquids are distilled and thereby separated for purification. We also said that when a liquid tincture is being distilled, the energy part of it—the mercury or alcohol—is highly susceptible to energetic influences. Alchemists take advantage of this receptive state, combining it with the astral influences of planetary hours and their own consciousness as participant in the process, thereby increasing the energy level of the tincture.

However, water is very fragile as an energy transfer and storage medium. The energetic changes created in a vapor state hold because of the additions of the sulphur and salt and, in some instances, through the addition of gold or a diluted drop of the alchemist's blood. If it were not for these additional properties, the charged water would quickly dissipate its energy level. This can easily be seen in the rainwater alchemists seek to collect. Rain that is charged in the highly electric atmosphere of April and May, and preferably collected during a lightning storm, is highly prized. The famous prints in the alchemical treatise *Mutus Liber* show alchemists catching the morning dew on sheets and collecting it in wooden—presumably oak—buckets for use in the laboratory. Once collected, it was used quickly before its energy could deteriorate.

The healing power of fresh spring dew was also considered very beneficial for skin ailments. Traditional German folk magic encourages walking barefoot on the morning dew to keep the aura healthy and strong. In fact, in the Medieval and Renaissance traditions, any water that fell from heaven was considered exceptionally beneficial. Where it landed or how it was collected only added to its uniqueness. Water, snow, or even hail collected during the holy seasons, on holy ground, such as a churchyard or cemetery, or inside the hollow of an old oak were highly sought. The most beneficial of all was water collected on April 1, or the morning after Walpurgis Nacht. Because of its sacramental nature and use, baptismal water also gained favor in folk practices. It was also believed that you could make holy water by placing written pieces of scripture inside previously unblessed or unconsecrated water that had been collected in the above fashions. Since drawing down the power of the Full Moon into a chalice of water or wine is a standard Wiccan rite, as is the exposure of crystals, talismans, and mirrors to the rays of the Moon, we can presume that it would be advantageous to collect water during the New Moon and Full Moon cycles as well.

Experiments conducted at McGill University in Montreal have demonstrated the ability of individuals to impact the energetic patterns of water and, using it as a medium, transfer those patterns to living organisms. In his groundbreaking work *Vibrational Medicine*,

Dr. Richard Gerber, M.D., describes the work done by Dr. Bernard Grad. The first set of experiments intended to see whether the energy field suggested by aura photography really existed and if this energy field could be made to assist in healing other human beings. To eliminate the placebo effect, or the patient's own positive belief system in regard to being healed, Grad needed to create a sick patient that had no beliefs. He achieved this by using plants, specifically barley seeds soaked in salt water. (Salt water is a known growth retardant.) Grad then had self-described "healers" perform a "laying on of hands" on the container of saline solution. Lab assistants then placed the barley seeds into a container holding the healer-treated water. Salt water untreated by the healers was used as a control.

After soaking in the saline solution, the seeds were placed in incubators and watched for signs of growth or signs of deterioration caused by their exposure to salt water. At the end of his study, Grad found that the seeds exposed to the healer-treated water sprouted at a higher rate than those soaked in untreated water and that, upon planting, they grew to greater height and had higher chlorophyll content. Grad performed this experiment again, using psychiatric patients as a variable, and found that water held by severely depressed patients dramatically reduced sprouting and growth rates. Grad's chemical analysis of healer-treated water using infrared spectroscopy demonstrated that the surface tension of the water was significantly decreased, along with a decrease in hydrogen bonding, compared to untreated water.[1]

Given that our physical bodies are 90 percent water, the idea that water can be charged with specific emotional and thought patterns that in turn affect other living organisms is a critical one for practical occultists.

---

1 Richard Gerber, *Vibrational Medicine* (Santa Fe, NM: Bear and Co., 1996), 77–78.

PSYCHIC EXPERIMENTS WITH WATER

Alchemy, Qabala, and astrology all point to a close relationship between the Moon and water. The Moon has powerful effects on our aura and, as such, our mental and physical health. The following experiment is beneficial in expanding and strengthening the aura and awakening the psychic centers. You can do it frequently, even daily, without any ill effects. In addition, with a few minor variations, it is an experiment that you can do with others, thereby testing the results in an objective fashion.

Charging Water

1. Prepare yourself for meditation with several minutes of slow, deep breathing.

2. Hold a glass of cold water in your hands, six inches to a foot in front of your solar plexus.[2] Place your fingers and thumb over the rim if possible.

3. Breathe in slowly, hold your breath, and imagine a brilliant bluish white or silver light moving through your arms and into the water. Image a brilliant sphere of light forming about the glass. Hold this image for a minute or two, and then dismiss it and simply breathe, focusing your breath on the glass as you exhale.

4. Continue breathing in this manner for three to five minutes, longer if you like, and then drink the water. It can also be poured on houseplants, given to pets, or drunk by another in your household who may be sick.

5. Record your experiences in your notebook.

---

2   "The colder water is, the greater is its accumulative capacity. With its full specific weight, namely 39 degrees F (4°C), it is most responsive. . . . Up to 43°F (6°C) [the difference] is insignificant. . . . Between 97–99°F (36–37°C) it [water] becomes neutral to magnetism." Franz Bardon, *Initiation into Hermetics* (Salt Lake City: Merkur Publishing, Inc., 2001), 60.

This experiment is best done in a dark room, where your aura may begin to collect and glow brightly around the glass and your hands. It is best to hold the glass slightly farther out from your body as described, rather than closer in, so that the energy that collects in your solar plexus can be pulled out to charge the water as well. This causes the aura to expand and increase in size, health, and vitality.

Charging Water with an Element

In *Initiation into Hermetics*, Franz Bardon (1909–1958), a Czech occultist, describes how water can be charged with the elements and how its taste should change accordingly. Bardon is one of the leading occult figures of the twentieth century, and, while authoring only three books, he demonstrates a comprehensive knowledge of several occult traditions and gives detailed instructions for their mastery. His works have been used by a variety of occult and esoteric groups, including Wicca, often without acknowledgment.[3] According to Bardon, the taste of elementally charged water should change according to the element used, and this change can be measured using litmus paper. This experiment is the same as the above, except you will use a single element to imbue a specific quality to the water. The more familiar you are with the elements, the greater will be your results.

1. Prepare yourself for meditation with several minutes of slow, deep breathing.

2. Hold a glass of cold water in your hands, six inches to a foot in front of your solar plexus. Place your fingers and thumb over the rim if possible.

3. Breathe in slowly, hold your breath, and imagine a brilliant bluish white or silver light moving through your arms and into the water. Image a brilliant sphere of light forming about the glass. Hold this image for a minute or two.

---

3 John Michael Greer, *The New Encyclopedia of the Occult* (St. Paul, MN: Llewellyn Publications, 2004), 59–60.

4. Change the image or sensation you are focusing on to the specific element you want to charge the water with. You may combine color with your visualization; however, emotional focus and kinesthetic qualities are most important in this experiment. Hold the image for several minutes, and then dismiss it and simply breathe, focusing your breath on the glass as you exhale.

5. Continue breathing in this manner for three to five minutes, longer if you like, and then drink the water. You may do this experiment in a group and then sample each other's water to see if there is any noticeable change in its texture, taste, or other overall qualities.

6. Record your experiences in your notebook.

Charging Water with Sound

Sound is connected to breath and rhythmic breathing. Without breath, there is no sound. Without controlled and measured breathing, singing and chanting could not be done. Hermeticism is replete with references to the power of sound and to voices human and divine to create. The vibrations set in motion by chanting divine names is well known in Qabala and can be easily applied here as well. The Gnostic divine name IAO, used widely in several Western traditions, is made up completely of vowels, making it ideal for this experiment.

1. Prepare yourself for meditation with several minutes of slow, deep breathing.

2. Hold a glass of cold water in your hands, six inches to a foot in front of your solar plexus. Place your fingers and thumb over the rim if possible.

3. Breathe in slowly, hold your breath, and imagine a brilliant bluish white or silver light moving through your arms and into the water. Image a brilliant sphere of light forming about the glass. Hold this image for a minute or two.

4. Hold the image for several minutes, and then dismiss it.

5. Breathe in, hold it, and chant "IAO" (pronounced "Eeee-Aaahhh-Oooohhh"). Feel the vibration moving through your whole body, and out your solar plexus in particular. Pause for a moment when you are done, then repeat the intonation two more times.

6. Continue breathing slowly and deeply for three to five minutes, longer if you like, and then drink the water. You may do this experiment in a group and then sample each other's water to see if there is any noticeable change in its texture, taste, or other overall qualities.

7. Record your experiences in your notebook.

DISTILLATION OF WATER

Distilled water is used in alchemy both to make products and to ingest them. While you can purchase distilled water commercially, it is good to get in the habit of making a few ounces in the beginning of your studies so that you can see how the process works. It is also a safe and easy introduction to the techniques of distillation.

Equipment Needed

The equipment needed is identical to that listed in the previous chapter. Several ounces of tap or spring water will be used in place of a tincture.

The Technique

The technique is identical to that described in the previous chapter. Place the water into the retort, or the large round-bottomed flask. Bring it to a very low boil. Continue until almost all of the water is out of the flask. Trace minerals that were present in the water will be left behind in your flask. Once you have completed distilling a few ounces of water, you may taste it and compare it to commercially prepared distilled water. You can also test both waters with litmus paper to see if there are any comparable changes in your homemade distilled water compared to the store brand.

SCENTED WATER AND WATER ELIXIRS

Once you are familiar with the basic technique of distilling water, you can move on to making simple and interesting Elixirs and scented waters from herbs. These will not have the same power as spagyric products made from alcohol, but with careful attention and the utilization of planetary hours, they can be made to have a noticeable energetic enhancement above a simple tea or herbal infusion.

The power of smell should not be easily dismissed, as it relates to the most ancient and primitive part of our brains and is linked to psychic phenomena of the highest order. The pituitary gland, so critical to psychic functioning and the gateway to spiritual Illumination, is situated in the brain at a point above the palate that allows it to be directly affected by breathing. Memory is intimately connected to scent, and despite the degrading of our olfactory senses by excessive use of crude commercially produced products, occultists rely on the power of incense to create immediate changes in their emotional and mental environment for rituals and meditation. An extensive array of emotional and mental associations and ancient memories can easily be brought forth by making a simple pass by the perfume counter in a department store or taking a morning walk past a church that uses incense. Nothing is stronger at inducing emotional evocation than smell.

For scented waters, it is important to pick a plant with a copious amount of essential oils. However, if this is not possible, the water-soluble oils that are released can be recouped and collected. The amount of oils is small; however, it is quality and not quantity that we are looking for.

In addition to lemon balm, several herbs of importance to the alchemist because of their attributes of providing for health and long life are sage and juniper berries. Part of this is due to the chemical properties of these plants, but the more important reason is the concentration of specific qualities of life force that result when placing lemon balm and sage under Jupiter and juniper berries under Mars (and Aries), although sometimes the Sun. Traditional herbal and alchemical medicine and modern medicine have yet to agree on many things, and before ingesting any herbal product, is it best to consult a health care provider who specializes in alternative and natural medicines to ensure that you will not have an allergic reaction.

The Technique

1. Read all directions several times prior to undertaking the experiment. Be sure you are familiar with every step of the process prior to actually performing it. Remember: Safety first!

2. Grind your herb to as small and fine particles as possible. Use a clean coffee grinder if needed when dealing with harder dried herbs such as pine needles or berries.

3. Place the ground herb into your large flask and pour enough distilled water in to cover the herb completely. Soak the herb for twenty-four hours. Measure the amount of water used so that you will recognize when it has gone over into the receiving flask.

4. Place the large flask over its heat source. Do not allow the water to boil. Watch as white steam clouds begin to form in the upper chamber.

5. When all of the water has come over, leave the large flask on the heat source for five minutes; then remove it and allow it to cool.

6. Using a wooden, glass, or plastic dowel or spoon, scrape the herbal mass at the bottom clean. Do not use metal, as it will scratch the glass and weaken it. Grind the mass with a mortar and pestle and place it back into the large flask.

7. Remove any white or dark oil spots that may be floating on top of the distillate. Place them in a small jar for later use.

8. Pour the distillate back into the large flask, mix it with the ground herb, and repeat the process. Leave the flask on the heat source for five minutes after all of the liquid has gone

over to the small receiving flask; then remove it and allow it to cool.

9. Repeat steps 6 through 8 for a total of seven rounds. After the fourth round, increase the time the large flask is left on the heat after the distillate has gone over to the small flask from five minutes to ten to fifteen minutes.

10. After the seventh round, calcine your herb, which by now will have already begun the process during the exposure to prolonged heat.

11. Purify the salt to as fine a color as possible and recombine it with the fluid you have collected. This is now your alchemical tincture using distilled water.

It is important that you pay close attention to the temperature of your heat source, as the alchemists of old worked at low temperatures to preserve the life force of the plant. This life force is what alchemists seek to capture, concentrate, and use in their healing and spiritual work.

KEY POINTS

- Water is the chief means of transferring energy in alchemy.
- Folklore is filled with examples of collecting and using water for healing and magical purposes that parallel Hermeticism.
- It has been scientifically proven that thoughts and feelings can affect the energetic nature of water and whatever the charged water comes into contact with.
- Water can be charged through visualization, sound, planetary hours, or herbs.
- Distilled water is used in the creation and ingestion of many spagyric products.

General Assignments for Chapter Five

1. Practice the exercises outlined in this chapter and record your experiences in your notebook.

2. Charge water, have someone drink it, and ask if there was any change in texture or taste.

3. Charge water and use it to maintain your houseplants.

4. Purchase three roses and place them in separate vases. Use charged water for one and tap water for the second, and for the third rose, add the nutrient powder supplied by florists to the water. Compare the life span of the three flowers and record the results in your notebook.

5. Distill several ounces of water and make an herbal tincture with it.

Meditation Practices for Chapter Five

There are no specific meditations for this chapter. Practice the psychic experiments as outlined and record your experiences. Pay attention to the lunar cycles and your dreams as you undertake these experiments.

six

INITIATIC ALCHEMY

According to Paracelsus, the *Ens* is among the most powerful and easiest medicines to make. The Ens is an *influence*, or principle that affects us and is a definite spiritual, psychic, or physical thing. While five such principles are designated as creating illness within

us, the Ens tincture, created from the vegetable kingdom, can be used to correct these imbalances and bring us physical and psychic health. In addition, the Ens allows a means of working in the plant realm toward specifically initiatic products. According to spagyric theory, the Ens manifests the highest initiatic virtue of the plant it created.

It is this initiatic aspect we seek when we create and ingest the Ens of a particular plant. Authorities seemingly disagree on the nature of spagyric medicines when it comes to this point. At least one authority claims that initiation is the sole goal of the alchemical product. Others, particularly Frater Albertus, Bacstrom, and Manfred Junius, suggest that powerful medicines for physical illnesses may be produced using the alchemical process. A middle ground has also been offered (and has been stated in a previous chapter): that the creator of the product realizes more of a spiritual benefit from its ingestion, while another may realize more of a physical benefit from its use. Hermetic tradition supports this middle position as well as the possibility of the recipient, who has not assisted in the medicine's creation, reacting much more strongly at the sudden increase in overall vibratory rate. Some individuals who have taken alchemical products are said to have responded violently to ingesting unprepared the more potent metallic and mineral medicines. As a qualifier, it might be that the effects of the medicine will cause anyone who does not involve themselves in spiritual or esoteric activities on a regular basis to find either a more physical reaction or a more violent shock.

INITIATION

The nature of esoteric initiation is often misconstrued by students, and even often by those who would pretend to grant it, either through rituals, by oral transmission, or in so-called astral or psychic initiations. It is sufficient to say initiation is the beginning of a new aspect of our interior development. One may have interior experiences without initiation, of course; however, initiation sets them apart by making them progressive in their function, intensity, and purpose. The role of initiation is to assist us in having and understanding our inner development. This, however, can be a bit of a stumbling block. Many schools, orders, and societies offer initiations into their various degrees, complete with beautiful rituals, titles, and whatnot. However, students of alchemy will most likely have realized by the time they begin their alchemical studies that these exterior initiations are but ritualized shadows, imitations and promises of things to come. True and lasting initiation is only had from within.

The words of eighteenth-century French mystic and philosopher Louis Claude de St. Martin are in perfect harmony with the alchemical vision of initiation:

> The only initiation which I preach and seek with all the ardour of my soul is that by which we may enter into the heart of God and make God's heart enter into us, there to form an indissoluble marriage, which will make us the friend, brother, and spouse of our divine Redeemer. There is no other mystery to arrive at this holy initiation than to go more and more down into the depths of our being, and not

let go till we can bring forth the living vivifying root, because then all the fruit . . . will be produced within us and without us naturally.[1]

But then we ask: Are the two always separate? Are all external rituals essentially poor imitations of an interior state? By no means is that an absolute. Unfortunately, for a ritual initiation to work—that is, to have its intended effect—the initiator must be higher in psychic vibration than the one receiving the psychic impulse. In our modern society, this is rarely the case.

Since alchemy has no set rituals, no lodges, and no methods of advancement other than the work itself, all initiation is said to be interior in this form of esotericism. We initiate ourselves into the work, and the work initiates us into higher (and deeper) levels of consciousness. To those who would object to this statement, ponder just this one question: Are we not always our own initiator? That is, are we not solely responsible for our starting, progressing, and finishing the path? Is it not our own Higher Selves that prompt us onward? It is from this Higher Self that in meditation, dreams, and sudden flashes of lucidity we are initiated—initiated, that is, back into the presence of our True Selves, the center and origin of our Being.

In this light, an initiation may come completely devoid of ritual or ceremony. It may be a sudden event that changes us completely. It may even be a veritable incarnation of a Qabalistic or alchemical pathworking, unfolding in daily life. In the end, however, as the word implies, initiation is only the beginning of the new stage of development, and that phase is only completed when we have been initiated into the next phase at the hand of our Interior Master, our very soul. It does us little good to go around collecting ritual initiations at the hands of would-be or even authentic masters, as these are not things that one can hang on the wall like a diploma. It is best

---

1 Edward Burton Penny, ed. and trans., *Theosophic Correspondence Between Louis Claude de Saint-Martin (The "Unknown Philosopher") and Kirchberger, Baron de Liebistorf (Member of the Grand Council of Berne)* (Pasadena, CA: Theosophical University Press, 1949), http://www.theosociety.org/pasadena/stmartin/stm-hp.htm (accessed July 7, 2006).

if we focus our energies on a singular path and complete it instead of running around looking for shortcuts and getting nowhere.

As egos seeking spiritual realities, we can only prepare ourselves for initiation, present ourselves at the door of the interior temple, and knock. It is said, "Knock and it shall be opened to you; ask and it shall be given." We may knock, ask, and wait in patience and silence, but never demand. True interior initiation comes but once, for that is all that is needed, creating within us a permanent change in consciousness—a permanent change that is at once expansive, unitarian, comprehensive, and evolutionary in nature. It is an ever-expanding upward spiral of what Israel Regardie called Light, Life, Love, Law, and Liberty.

How many initiations we experience is dependent upon our chosen path, be it alchemical, Qabalistic, Wiccan, or Neopagan. But even here, the idea of division is more of a function of our exterior consciousness than our interior awareness. We consume both spiritual food and material food in small doses so that we do not choke or get indigestion, yet at the end of the meal, all of the needed food for our growth and survival is consumed. Initiation is the same, in that it is a small chunking of a larger piece of life consciousness. We receive in interior initiation exactly what we need for our growth—no more, no less. How many of these small spoonfuls of life we swallow depends on our chosen interior path and the degree of progress we make on it. Thus, once again, the obligation and responsibility is ours.

In summary, it might be said that we can be expected to experience an initiation for each plane of awareness, and one for each of its subplanes. How this works out mathematically is up for debate. One school of thought suggests that there are twelve planes: seven major and five minor, with each having its own subdivision of five planes, for a total of sixty levels of Being progressively available to us. However, each time we experience an initiation, there is in reality only One Being that is experienced, and our awareness of that One is expanded. To be overly concerned with levels of initiation before it is revealed is to feed the ego and not the soul.

Some Hermetic schools that use the Tree of Life suggest that just as the sphere of Malkuth (physical life) is composed of the four elements synthesized by *Quintessentia*, or Spirit, each of the remaining nine spheres also has four subplanes, with a single unifying plane at the end. Thus, each sphere of the Tree of Life can be said to have its own earth, water, air, fire, and Spirit aspects. This is why it is possible to create a specialized plant or mineral product designed to affect the fire, air, water, or earth energy of the planets or psychic centers they are associated with. Through a fire product, such as the Ens, we affect consciousness directly. An air product, such as an Elixir that is "exhaled," affects the mind as well as organizing ability and energy patterns. A water product, such as a spagyric tincture, affects the astral energies, while an earth product affects the etheric and material bodies directly. Mineral products are powerful healers because of their earth nature, as are spagyric products made primarily of plant roots. However, since these elements are also organized in a hierarchy of subtle to dense, as well as organically, impacting fire has a ripple effect across the remaining elements. Impacting water affects earth and, if strong enough, may have an effect on air. While we seek to compartmentalize ideas for the sake of understanding and technical application, Nature is not so neat and discrete. This subtle relationship cannot be memorized, only understood through direct experience—the kind of experience that alchemy can offer.

The nature of spagyric tinctures, and in particular the Ens, is to clear out the blocks in our psychic makeup and anatomy, similar to what is called *nadis* in yoga or the *meridians* in acupuncture. This subtle anatomy allows for the exchange of information between the dense physical world of matter, the endpoint of creation, and the subtler psychic world, of which it is an extension. In creation, there are no breaks, gaps, or holes; such exist only in our knowledge or realization of Nature. By effecting change on this subtle in-between level, we can increase the flow and quality of energy from these slightly finer worlds "above" to our physical world "below." With each corresponding increase in intensity, an initiation can be said to have taken place if, of course, the energy becomes permanently available to us and the increase is not just a temporary jump to a higher level. These psychic nerve channels exist in the planet as well as in humanity, in the form of ley lines.

As stated in chapter 1, alchemists call the natural power of creation the Secret Fire.[2] It is the force that continually changes all of creation, moving it forward to more and more refined levels. When we create and ingest spagyric or alchemical products, we are assisting Nature in the quickening of our personal evolutionary process.

The Secret Fire works on the etheric levels. All substances and all elements have their bases in this prematter we call the etheric, and as such, they can be approached from the level of the invisible if you know how to adjust and direct the Secret Fire. This "fire" gives us power and control over what is often called inanimate nature. In truth, nothing is really inanimate, as life exists in all matter to some degree. In a rock's consciousness, life is in a deep trance; in the vegetable realm, it sleeps; in the animal realm, it stirs; and it becomes self-aware degree by degree in humanity.

Like our basic tincture previously described, an Ens tincture can be made for each of the seven planetary rulers for each day of the week. It is through the herb influenced by a particular planet that we seek initiation into the Qabalistic sphere or world ruled by that planet. However, unlike a Plant Stone, the Ens has a lesser initiatic power, although it is still quite surprising. In the Plant Stone, the four aspects or elements of earth, air, water, and fire are in balance. In the Ens, the fire element is predominant, for reasons we shall see. The advantage lies in the simplicity of its creation, allowing anyone, regardless of experience level, to create an Ens tincture.

From another perspective, the Ens may be seen as comparable to Elixirs in which the tincture has been "exalted" through repeated processing and in which the tincture's calcined salts have been added to the procedure. However, Elixirs almost always contain several species of plants as well.

---

2 *Aesch Mezareph*, or "Purifying Fire," is the Hebrew equivalent, and is also the name of an alchemical manuscript.

How to Make an Ens

While several methods exist for the creation of the Ens, the one described here is easy and safe and requires no special equipment. While herbs freshly cut immediately before use are preferred, they can be cut several days beforehand and stored in a plastic container in your refrigerator to maintain freshness. The glass used in making an Ens will be etched by the caustic nature of the liquefied potassium carbonate; therefore, use materials that you will set aside for use only in making future Ens.

Equipment Needed
- Glass jar or container for making a tincture. Canning jars work best.
- 1 ounce of dried plant, or preferably 2 or more ounces of herb.
- 1½ pounds of potassium carbonate.
- Glass dish no less than one inch deep.

Technique for Making an Ens
1. Read all directions several times prior to undertaking the experiment. Be sure that you are familiar with the process prior to its actual performance.

2. Spread the potassium carbonate in a thin layer inside the glass dish, no more than a quarter of an inch thick (less than 1 centimeter). Take caution to avoid exposure to the potassium carbonate in either its dry state or when it becomes liquefied through exposure to the night air, as it is toxic and can cause a rash or burning of the mucous membranes. Wash your hands thoroughly after handling it to avoid any accidental exposure or contamination of your eyes or other sensitive areas. Remember, the potassium carbonate will etch the sides of the glass container used during this experiment.

3. Place the tray in an area where it will be exposed to the night air. As potassium carbonate (or salt of tartar) liquefies (becomes

deliquescent), it absorbs the water carried in the night air. This water, or humidity, is the vehicle of Universal Fire, It is most easily obtained in the spring and summer months and is known as "Angel Water."

4. Decant or filter off the liquid each morning, being sure to avoid its exposure to the sun or a direct water source, such as rain. To do this, use either a syringe, large eyedropper, turkey baster, or lab pipette set aside only for this purpose, as it will also be etched by the Angel Water.

5. *Caution:* Never pipette by mouth!

6. When 4 to 5 ounces (125 to 150 milliliters) have been collected, you can begin the first Ens tincture. To avoid too much loss of this precious liquid through filtering, you may want to collect it in a jar or flask and then filter it all at once prior to use. Note: It will etch the glass it is stored in just as it does the container that is used to make it.

7. Make sure you seal the storage jar tightly to prevent the liquid from absorbing any additional fluid from the surrounding air. Fill only two-thirds of the jar, leaving room for possible expansion if the seal is accidently loosened or broken.

8. Place an ounce of finely ground herb, or several ounces of freshly cut herb, in a fresh jar and pour in the clear fluid you have collected and filtered on the planetary day and/or hour of the planet ruling the herb. Pour in enough fluid to cover the top of the herb and to allow for thorough shaking. Depending on the absorbent nature of the herb chosen, this can be from 100 to 200 milliliters of the collected "Oil of Tartar" per herb for adequate coverage. If any Oil of Tartar remains, save it for future use.

9. Pour in an equal amount of grain alcohol and shake daily to ensure the two liquids mix, as the lighter alcohol will float on top. The alcohol that forms the Ens tincture is removed after it turns a dark reddish color. It will only take on the color

and tincture of the Oil of Tartar through repeated mixing, as the two fluids will quickly separate.

10. When you have obtained the proper color, pipette the top layer of alcohol off and store it separately. It is ready for use. (You can use a turkey baster set aside exclusively for this purpose.)

11. Be careful not to pull off any of the Oil of Tartar, as it is caustic and will be very unpleasant if swallowed.

Because of the magnetic nature of the deliquescence, it is important that the lid be nonmetallic or that the mouth of the jar be wrapped in plastic food wrap prior to sealing. You may also wish to wrap it in aluminum foil to limit or reduce the amount of psychic contact the liquid receives.

USING THE ENS

Take ten or at most twenty drops in a glass of preferably distilled water on the day ruled by the planet of the plant in the hour following sunrise. If this is not possible, then take it in any of the other three planetary hours occurring that day. As before, you may consecrate it prior to consumption with Qabalistic or astrological rituals, as you would do for a talisman.

Because the Ens is an initiatic product, it will have an effect on the subtle or astral body of the user. Note carefully your dreams in your notebook, as well as the phases of the Moon and any other psychic or coincidental occurrences that may happen.

This Universal Fire is what sets both our personal and planetary energy, or Secret Fire, into action on various levels. This is the *kundalini* energy of yoga that is carried in the vital energy of the air, or *prana*. This is the *only* energy that can initiate into the spiritual realms.

Those with Qabalistic training or experience in ritual magic will see a similarity in the idea presented here with the elemental attributes of the so-called magic circle. The Universal Fire (also known as *Ruach* in Hebrew and *Spiritus* in Latin) is the vital life energy carried in the air (spring, the east), from which we extract the vital principle or experience it as fire (summer, the south) by means of water (autumn, the west) and capture it in the physical medium of the earthly herb (winter, the north).

For those not wishing to create all seven of the Ens at once, take the following into consideration when picking a plant for your first time: you may pick a plant based upon its planetary sign, such as one for a quality that you are deficient in. (Qabalists take note, as spagyric tinctures can be used to facilitate specific rituals and Paths.)

A Moon Ens will open up the psychic world (Yetzirah and Yesod in particular). It may also be used with pathworkings involving the Moon, the 32nd, 30th, 28th, and 25th Paths on the Tree of Life (see the diagram on the opposite page).

- An Ens of lady's mantle (*Alchemilla vulgaris*) will open up Venus (Netzach) and give information regarding plant alchemy, hence its official name *Alchemilla*.

- An Ens of eyebright will assist in awakening intuition and inner communion. It may even give glimpses of the World of Archetypes and the Higher Mind (Briatic World). It may also be used in rituals and pathworkings involving the Sun.

- An Ens of Saturn, particularly horsetail, may be used in the 32nd Path and opening of Saturn and may even give glimpses of the Archetypal World and Eternity itself. This is a very powerful product and should be the first we make to clean our psychic channels and open ourselves to increased levels of energy and consciousness.

In his biography of Paracelsus, Franz Hartmann quotes an unknown manuscript, allegedly in private possession, in which Paracelsus described the creation of the Melissa Ens and its virtues:

But the Primum Ens Melissae is prepared in the following manner: Take half a pound of pure carbonate of potash, and expose it to the air until it is dissolved (by attracting water from the atmosphere).

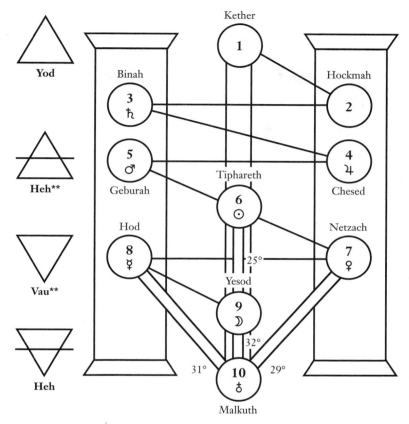

*First paths of initiation into alchemy and Qabala
**The order of the elements on the Tree according to alchemy

Tree of Life*

Filter the fluid, and put as many fresh leaves of the plant into it as it will hold, so that the fluid will cover the leaves. Let it stand in a well-closed glass and in a moderately warm place for twenty-four hours. The fluid may then be removed from the leaves, and the latter thrown away. On top of this fluid absolute alcohol is poured, so that it will cover the former to the height of one or two inches, and it is left to remain for one or two days, or until the alcohol becomes of an intensely green color. This alcohol is then to be taken away and preserved, and fresh alcohol is put upon the alkaline fluid, and the operation is repeated until all the coloring matter is absorbed by the alcohol. This alcoholic fluid is now to be distilled, and the alcohol evaporated until it becomes of the thickness of a syrup, which is the Primum Ens Melissae; but the alcohol that has been distilled away and the liquid potash may be used again. The liquid potash must be of great concentration and the alcohol of great strength, else they would become mixed, and the experiment would not succeed.[3]

In a footnote to the above material, Hartmann quotes Lesebure, a physician of Louis XIV of France, and his *Guide to Chemistry* (printed in Nuremburg in 1685, page 276), in which Lesebure describes the following account of an experiment he claims to have witnessed regarding the extended use of the Primum Ens Melissae:[4]

One of my most intimate friends prepared the Primum Ens Melissae, and his curiosity would not allow him to rest until he had seen with his own eyes the effects of this arcanum, so that he might be certain whether or not the accounts given of its virtues were true. He therefore made the experiment, first upon himself, then upon an old female servant, aged seventy years, and afterwards upon an old hen that was kept at his house. First he took, every morning at sunrise, a glass of white wine that was tinctured with this remedy, and after using it for fourteen days his finger- and toe-nails began to fall out, without, however, causing any pain. He was not courageous enough to continue the experiment, but gave the same remedy to the old female servant. She took it every morning for about ten days, when she began to menstruate again as in former days. At this she was very much surprised, because she did not know that she had been taking a medicine. She became frightened, and refused to continue the experiment. My friend took, therefore, some grain, soaked it in that wine, and gave it to the old hen to eat, and on the sixth day that bird began to lose its feathers, and kept losing them until it was perfectly nude, but before two weeks had passed, new feathers grew, which were much more beautifully colored; her comb stood up again, and she began again to lay eggs.[5]

---

3 Franz Hartmann, *The Life of Philippus Theophrastus, Bombast of Hohenhem* (London: G. Redway, 1887), 210.

4 The lemon balm must be collected before a Full Moon in May or November (Gemini and Sagittarius respectively) and dried, and the Ens begun with the Moon waxing.

5 Ibid.

According to one modern manuscript on alchemy, a similar experiment using a different method of extraction produced a milder and less violent reaction in the hens it was given to, while increasing their egg weight and production.

While this is not being related to encourage extended use of the tincture, it is from stories such as these that we know of the legendary healing and rejuvenating qualities of alchemical products.

KEY POINTS

- Alchemical initiation is defined as personal, interior, and progressive changes in consciousness that may be manifested externally as increasingly powerful transmutations and an increase in life energy.

- Qabalistic cosmology as expressed in the Tree of Life can assist in understanding the pattern and purpose of alchemical initiations.

- These initiations progress from the densest psychic realms of the Moon to the subtlest of Saturn, into Unity itself.

- The four elements and the Quintessence exist in the material world and also form substrata of each of the planetary levels, as expressed by the spheres on the Tree of Life.

- Spagyric products help clear the psychic channels (or *nadis* in yoga and *meridians* in acupuncture).

- The etheric matrix is the "Secret Fire" of the material world, the serpent of *kundalini*. Through progressive cleansing of the etheric channels, the Secret Fire is naturally brought into conscious operation.

- A dream notebook is essential in understanding our inner experiences.

GENERAL ASSIGNMENTS FOR CHAPTER SIX

1. Create an Ens for each of the seven ancient planets.

2. Draw the polygon or geometric shape for each of the seven ancient planets and place the corresponding planetary symbol in the center. Draw them in black on white or in their planetary colors on white. They can also be drawn in their complementary color on their primary background. For example, the color for Mars is red, so the pentagon or pentagram with the symbol for Mars would be drawn in green on a red surface. These polygons can be found in Israel Regardie's *The Golden Dawn*, John Michael Greer's *Circles of Power*, and Jean Dubuis's *Fundamentals of Esotericism*.

MEDITATION PRACTICES FOR CHAPTER SIX

Daily Planetary Meditations

Meditate on the principal planet using the drawing you have made. As you progress, visualize the images in color as you have made them. When meditating, visualize the image at the nape of your neck, where the head sits on the spinal column. Hold the image as if you were looking back through your skull at it, and imagine it as a brilliant, glowing "etheric tattoo." Do this meditation particularly during the appropriate planetary hour for each of the polygons.

Lucid Dreaming

Using the method outlined above, visualize the polygon with its planetary symbol in the center at the nape of your neck as you fall asleep. This will induce dreaming and lucid dreaming. Write down your experiences in your notebook.

Initiation

Meditate on the nature of initiation and how a permanent change in your consciousness in one or more specific areas would benefit you. Consider what you need to do to facilitate that change.

The Philosopher's Stone

Meditate on the nature of the Philosopher's Stone, what it means to you, and what you are doing to "fix" or incarnate those ideals in your daily life. Carry a small picture or drawing of the "Stone" and remind yourself of these ideals and your commitment at regular times each day.

seven

PHYSICAL HEALTH AND HEALING WITH SPAGYRICS

WHY WE SEEK HEALTH

For many, the alchemical path begins because they are seeking gold; for others, long life; and for some, to heal themselves or those they love of sickness. In the end, all undertake the alchemical journey with the hope—better still, the burning desire—to end pain and suffering in their lives

or for others. Even in its most basic aspect, the desire for long life (if not immortality) and infinite riches has, at its root, the desire to end suffering in some form. This is important, because all of these aspects—wisdom, wealth, health, and the power and responsibility they bring—are under the domain of Jupiter.

These four properties of Jupiter—health, wealth, wisdom, and power—can be interpreted as the four elemental qualities of Jupiter. Health is water, wisdom is air, wealth is earth, and power is fire. Combined and in harmony, they represent the divine plan, or the blueprint for our life as we imagine it. Yet there is a trick. These very things we seek, we cannot seek for ourselves alone, but for all of humanity. Our actions must be based in a broad and tolerant love—but not foolish or incredulous—and we must seek to be of service to the greater evolution of all life.

To be an alchemist, a true alchemist of this level, is to undertake the equivalent of the Bodhisattva's vow, wherein we live to assist others in their becoming, and not for any purely selfish reasons.

In this respect, we cannot seek health simply because we do not wish to be sick or because we are afraid of death. Health is our natural and active state, and it must be maintained by kind, loving, and generous thoughts, feelings, and actions. If we are to live and be supported by this planet, we need to demonstrate that our continued life is of value. We need to demonstrate that we are more than just eating, sleeping, and sensation-seeking machines, but rather that we can integrate the highest values with the most basic acts and be an example of practical spirituality to those around us. In harmonizing our outer life with our innermost dreams, we experience health and life as a natural expression of who we are. Alchemists use plant and mineral products to help achieve this state of harmony and, with it, reflect the Hermetic axiom "As above, so below."

PROBLEMS OF DOSAGE

The diagnosis of a disease and prescription of treatment for it is the business of medicine. It is important to recognize that it is illegal to practice medicine without a license. For this reason, if you are not a qualified medical practitioner, use the information in this chapter solely for education and do not attempt to treat anyone with spagyric products for physical illness. Experience is required in both the professional end of diagnosis as well as in the preparation of tinctures and assessing how much to ingest.

No disease affects every person identically. Each person will respond differently enough to the same disease that the same set of symptoms can be interpreted differently by several physicians, and only experience allows them to make proper diagnosis. Because spagyric products are increased in their potency with each operation of separation and recombination, the amount needed for a specific disease will differ not only with the patient, but also with the strength of the Elixir prescribed.

Tinctures are often taken diluted at one or two drops in a teaspoon of water or ten drops in a glass of water. Some will brave it and take it directly under the tongue as well. For physical illness, the drops are to be taken hourly, whereas for meditation, the tincture's dose is taken once a day or at specific weekly intervals.

The choice of herb is tricky, as some alchemists insist on the doctrine of correspondences, yet it is more common to take an herb based upon its healing properties in relationship to the disease and prepare or use it as the basis for a tincture. In this instance, it might be advisable to consult a homeopathic or naturopathic physician for herbal suggestions on which to base the production of an Elixir.

It is also unrealistic, despite the great potency of spagyric products, to expect to heal everything. It is not uncommon for people to turn to alternative forms of healing only at the end of their medical journeys rather than as a complement during allopathic treatment. This is unfortunate, as it creates a condition that is most often worse than if they had begun using spagyric products earlier. This sense of desperation intensifies and charges the healing environment, and it may create expectations that plant products are incapable of satisfying.

Spagyric products must be used:

- *Early*, to provide the optimum results;
- *Often*, that is, in small doses regularly rather than large doses at once; and
- *Correctly*, with the right tincture for the right disease.

If plant products are incapable of making any significant progress in curing the disease, then mineral products will need to be employed. Mineral products include either specific medicines made from specific minerals or products that have a broad power and influence, such as the White Stone or the Red Stone, two of the most important healing, rejuvenating, and spiritually initiating alchemical creations known in alchemy.

In his work *The Alchemist's Handbook*, Frater Albertus describes a method for testing the quality of a product:

> Before administering any alchemical medication to animals or sick individuals, a test should be performed to determine if the medicine is properly prepared. This is done by placing a small amount of the herbal substance on a thin sheet of heated copper. If it melts like wax and does not give off any smoke, and then solidifies again, it is an indication that the medication has been prepared correctly and that it is ready for use. . . . Alchemical herbal medications are the essence and salt in their purest form, as all irrelevant and extraneous matter has been removed during the process of calcinations. That which is essential cannot be destroyed by fire, but is only purified and brought to its preordained state.[1]

ALCHEMY AND HOMEOPATHY

The Spagyric Way of Preparing Medicine in Relationship to Parachemistry, a small pamphlet produced by Frater Albertus under his birth name, Albert Richard Riedel, Ph.D., hints at the relationship between alchemy and homeopathy when discussing mineral salts, an important part of alchemical and homeopathic treatments. Salts in spagyric products have the dual role of acting as a purifier (through filtration) for the energies of the plant and as an anchor for those same energies in the material world. Spagyrically prepared herbal products also owe part of their beneficial virtues to the mineral salts they contain. These salts are what are returned to the tincture after they are calcined. Even in instances in which the salt has not been calcined and a crude tincture is used, some of the mineral salts of the plant (known as "salts of the sulphur") will still be present. Mineral salts act in the same manner individually as when in a harmonic group with other salts or when found in herbs. Centuries of research on the actions of these salts and the symptoms produced by their deficiencies has led to their efficient use in affecting certain illnesses.

---

1 Frater Albertus, *The Alchemist's Handbook* (York Beach, ME: Weiser, 1987), 45–46.

These salts and their areas of action are:

Mineral Salt	Area of Symptomatic Relief
Aluminum Hydrate	Nervine for the sympathetic nervous system, stimulant
Antimony Sulfide, Golden	Depurative, stimulates circulation
Calcium Chloride	Restores elasticity, muscle weakness, muscle tonic
Calcium Fluoride	Blood vessels, tooth enamel, connective and elastic tissue, skin
Calcium Phosphate	Bones, general nutrition, digestive aid, tonic, antianaemic
Calcium Sulphate	Blood purifier, depurative, prevents cell disintegration and pus formation
Copper Sulphate	Thyroid, sexual organs, kidneys
Gold Chloride	Cardiac, tonic, heart, antiarthritic
Iron Phosphate	Reduces fever and inflammation, carries oxygen, antiphlogistic, antianaemic, febrifuge, haemostatic, vasotonic, vulnerary
Iron Sulphate	Depurative, gall bladder, antiphlogistic, blood oxygenation
Magnesium Phosphate	Antispasmodic, cardiac, spasm and cramp relaxative, carminative nervine
Mercury Chloride	Brain cell activator, liver cleanser, alternative, cholagogue, stimulant, hepatic, antisyphilitic
Potassium Chloride	Anticoagulant, depurative, hepatic, expectorant, mucus and clot neutralizer, cholagogue
Potassium Phosphate	Antiseptic, restorative, nervine, exanthemintic
Potassium Sulphate	Febrifuge, skin lubricant and opener, antiphlogistic, carminative, diaphoretic, exanthemintic, emmenagogue
Silic Oxide	Cleanser and eliminator, stimulates assimilation, depurative, diaphoretic, pus and tissue developer, maturing
Silver Chloride	Aids memory, brain tonic, antiseptic to mucus membranes
Sodium Chloride	Water distribution, promotes digestion, exanthemintic
Sodium Phosphate	Acid neutralizer, antacid, digestive, vermifuge, antirheumatic
Sodium Sulphate	Antibilious, cholagogue, depurative, water remover, hepatic, hydragogue
Zinc Chloride	Tissue and brain cell stimulant, astringent, antiseptic

The fundamental principle involved in the use of mineral salts is that of correcting a deficiency and, through that correction, establishing a harmony that results in "health" rather than seeking to achieve a specific result. This same fundamental process is carried over into homeopathy, which has its roots in alchemy.[2]

In 1873, Wilhelm Schuessler, a German homeopathic physician, proposed that of the salts found in the human body, the twelve major ones were responsible for maintaining health. Schuessler's ideas won adherents quickly and became very popular in Europe and even India. Like many forms of non-allopathic medicine, Schuessler's suffered during the second half of the twentieth century, but not before Dr. George Washington Carey and Inez Eudora Perry would adapt Schuessler's ideas into a complex form of esoteric healing very much in harmony with homeopathy's alchemical roots. Carey and Perry suggested that each of the twelve major cell salts found in the human body were related to one of the signs of the zodiac.[3]

From this basis, it has been theorized that since the number twelve is the basis for a complete life cycle (twelve months in the year, signs in the zodiac, gates of the New Jerusalem, Apostles, and Hebrew prophets), as well as the number of perfection in Renaissance numerology, the human body will always be missing a certain level of cell salts because its period of formation in the womb falls short of the number twelve. By the very fact that we take on physical life, we take on imperfection in form. Only through alchemical, homeopathic, or some other form of energetic means can this deficit be identified and corrected. The alchemical process for modifying these deficiencies is time consuming; however, a highly simplified variation of it, which follows, will assist in regaining energetic and physical well-being and maintaining health.[4]

---

2 For more on homeopathy, see: Elizabeth Danciger, *Homeopathy: From Alchemy to Medicine* (Rochester, VT: Healing Arts Press, 1987).

3 George Washington Carey and Inez Eudora Perry, *The Zodiac and the Salts of Salvation: Homeopathic Remedies for the Sign Types* (York Beach, ME: Weiser, 1996).

4 For the complete alchemical process, including the "Separation of the Waters," see lessons 25 and 26 in: Jean Dubuis, *Spagyrics: A Course in Plant Alchemy*, vol. 2 (Winfield, IL: Triad Publishing, n.d.). Available online at http://www.triad-publishing.com/Course_spg.html.

Sign	Mineral Salt	Cell Salt Name
Aries	Potassium Phosphate	Kali Phos
Taurus	Sodium Sulphate	Natrium Sulph
Gemini	Potassium Chloride	Kali Mur
Cancer	Fluoride of Lime	Calcium Fluoride
Leo	Magnesium Phosphate	Magnesium Phos
Virgo	Potassium Sulphate	Kali Sulph
Libra	Sodium Phosphate	Natrium Phos
Scorpio	Lime Sulphate	Calcium Sulph
Sagittarius	Silicea	Silicea
Capricorn	Lime Phosphate	Calcium Phos
Aquarius	Sodium Chloride	Natrium Mur
Pisces	Iron Phosphate	Ferrum Phos

Each sign also corresponds to a decant, or one-third, of other signs in its particular elemental grouping. For us, this means that one cell salt will be absent and several of the needed cell salts will always be low in our bodies, for a total of nine parts, or three decants for each of the missing three zodiacal signs if a fetus is carried to full term. If it is born prematurely, additional cell salts will be needed. To simplify the process of having to calculate which cell salts are needed, it is possible to obtain a single remedy that already contains all twelve cell salts. The following method uses this product:[5]

Method I

1. Collect rainwater, preferably in the months of April and May and during a lightning storm. Fresh snow can also be used if rainwater is not available.

2. Filter the water to remove any debris.

3. Dissolve nine tablets in 45 milliliters of rainwater.

4. Drink it.

---

5 Bioplasma is a combination of all twelve tissue remedies (cell salts) and is produced by P&S Laboratories, Los Angeles, CA 90061. They have been producing homeopathic products according to Dr. Schuessler's methods since 1903. Other companies may have similar products.

5. Do this daily for three months, starting with your birthday. If you were born prematurely, add additional weeks or months to compensate.

You will need a little over 4 liters of rainwater for this method.

Method II
Dissolve the pills in rainwater and circulate it at a very low heat, *or* allow it to digest for one month, preferably during the sign of Cancer.

Circulation Without a Laboratory
1. To circulate without a laboratory setup, place the liquid with the dissolved tablets in a glass container that is tall enough so that after the liquid is added, it will be at least three-quarters to four-fifths empty. Do this preferably on a Monday or Thursday morning during a New Moon or Full Moon.
2. Cover the mouth of the container with plastic food wrap and seal tightly.
3. Place on a low heat source for several hours. The liquid should never boil.
4. Allow it to cool before bottling.
5. Take 5 milliliters daily for three months, starting with your birthday.

Digestion
Digestion is the same as circulation, except that there is no external heat source pushing the product. For our purposes, time and astrological influences are the deciding factors. Start your operation on a Monday morning, on or near the New Moon, in the sign of Cancer or Virgo. Other signs can be used, but Cancer deals with growth and form of the body and Virgo rules the Sixth House, the house of health.

1. Place the liquid with the dissolved tablets in a glass container that is tall enough so that after the liquid is added, it will be at least three-quarters to four-fifths empty. An Erlenmeyer flask is ideal for this, as it has a long neck that allows for a great deal of evaporation and condensation of the liquid.

2. Stopper the flask or cover the mouth of the container with food wrap, sealing tightly.

3. Wrap the flask in aluminum foil. Cover it completely.

4. Allow it to sit in darkness for thirty or forty days.

5. Take 5 milliliters daily for three months, starting with your birthday.

You will need about 750 milliliters of rainwater for this method.

The addition of the highly charged rainwater (which can be kept in your refrigerator when not in use to hold the charge) and the extended period of digestion, allowing for "solve et coagula" to occur, is what makes this an alchemical product. Here we have three simple methods that can be followed with little or no equipment and that will give tremendous benefits toward improving physical health.

SALT STRUCTURES AND THE TREE OF LIFE

An extremely interesting but highly esoteric aspect of plant salts is that they also act in a manner reflecting their geometric shapes— shapes that have direct relationships to the planetary correspondences of the plants. Therefore, if we examine the calcined salt of a plant under a microscope, we will see that it has a specific shape and form. For example, salts of a cubic crystalline form relate to Saturn and can be used to assist in all areas in which the energies of Saturn are needed. This can be used to help us in deciding the correspondences for plants that are not listed in the traditional alchemical herbals.

This theory also demonstrates the Qabalistic theory of "Four Trees in Four Worlds," wherein the earth, or mineral, Tree is the first to form but the last to be animated with consciousness. Through the addition of mineral substances to our work, we not only anchor our work solidly in the material world, but also assist the mineral world in its evolution. The more we work with the salts of our plant products, the closer we bring the entire process into the realm of genuine alchemy, and by that we mean a transformative practice for both matter and energy.

Crystal	Planetary Correspondence of Plant	Sphere on the Tree of Life
Cubic	Saturn	Binah
Tetragonal	Jupiter	Chesed
Orthorhombic	Mars	Geburah
Monoclinic	Sun	Tiphareth
Triclinic	Venus	Netzach
Rhombohedral	Mercury	Hod
Hexagonal	Moon	Yesod

PLANETS, PLANTS, AND THEIR HEALING QUALITIES

Saturn

Saturn rules over: old age, chronic diseases, and life's lessons, or *karma*. Often perceived as the Cosmic Bookkeeper, Saturn is the planet of learning. If we have some introspection and self-discipline, Saturn will not be too difficult for us. If we lack these basic qualities, then we will perceive Saturn's influences as hostile, punitive, and even evil at times.

Saturn corresponds to: the bones, teeth, the spine (in conjunction with Leo), the spleen, hair, nails, all minerals in the body, joints and flexibility (especially the knees), and all slow and chronic activities of the body. Saturn governs age's hardening and restricting processes, such as the formation of crystals in the body as well as the hardening of the anterior lobe of the pituitary (restricting growth), hearing, memory, and circulation to the extremities and soft tissue.

Diseases associated with Saturn are: diseases affecting any of the above organs, including depression, melancholy, senility, crankiness, and lethargy; hardenings of the organs, arteries, or any calcification; rheumatism, arthritis, and anything chronic.

Plants associated with Saturn include:

Beta vulgaris—beetroot

Equisetum arvense—horsetail

Trigonella foenum-graecum—fenugreek

Hordeum—barley

Plantago coronopus—plantain

Polygonatum officinale—Solomon's seal

Secale cereale—rye

Sennia—senna

Symphytum officinale—comfrey (sometimes Jupiter)

Vinca minor—periwinkle, myrtle (sometimes lunar)

Viola tricolor—pansy

Zea mays—corn

Jupiter

Jupiter is the largest of the planets, the Sun being first, and bears many similarities to the Sun. Jupiter is in fact a sun that failed to fully ignite, and therefore it actually gives off more energy than it takes in. Jupiter is known as the Greater Benefic, and its placement in a birth chart is studied extensively because of the profound influences this planet has on so many significant areas of daily life. It is advisable to have a copy of your horoscope made so that you can study it in relation to the spagyric products you are making. If a planet is badly aspected, prepare a tincture for it.

Jupiter rules over: good health, wealth, philosophical and religious matters, ceremony, and the enjoyment of life.

Jupiter corresponds to: the liver, the lungs (sometimes with Mercury), arteries of the stomach and abdomen, digestion and assimilation of oxygen and nutrition, fatty tissues and areas of the body that store fat, the spleen (with Saturn), general antibiotic functions of the body, cell growth, general energy levels, and, in the brain, the occipital lobe of the pituitary body.

Diseases associated with Jupiter are: Jupiter does not promote disease but through its configuration with other planets can affect diseases, which include all diseases of excess and immoderation, particularly excessive drinking (Jupiter rules the liver), excessive eating, and even drug and substance abuse; congestion in the lungs, nose, and throat; poor blood (along with Mars); and the stomach. Jupiter has secondary effects on the heart and various cancers.

Plants associated with Jupiter include:

Agrimonia eupatoria—agrimony

Asparagus officinalis—asparagus

Borago officinalis—borage

Cichorium endivia—endive

Fraxinus ornus—manna, flowering ash

Inula helenium—elecampane (sometimes solar)

Melissa officinalis—lemon balm

Panax ginseng—ginseng

Rubus idaeus—raspberry

Salvia officinalis—sage

Symphytum officinale—comfrey (sometimes Saturn)

Vaccinium myrtillus—bilberry

Mars

Mars rules over: intense and often violent energy, bringing dynamic power to all that it encounters. Mars increases psychic ability as well as motion and power in the physical realm.

Mars corresponds to: the muscular system, male sexual organs, marrow, blood formation, the quality of red corpuscles, adrenaline (suprarenal glands), body heat and combustion, the gall bladder, and the purging of the body to maintain health.

Diseases associated with Mars are: swelling and inflammation of tissues, blood pressure (high and low), bleeding or any sudden and rapid onset of a disease, sharp pains, blisters, eruptions, and fevers. Mars also rules head injuries (via Aries) and the polarity between the sexual organs (Scorpio) and the brain (Aries), demonstrating the two terminals of the Secret Fire, or serpent energy.

Plants associated with Mars include:

Allium cepa—common onion

Allium sativum—garlic

Artemisia absinthium—wormwood

Capsicum—red pepper, paprika

Cochlearia armoracia—horseradish

Genista tinctoria—dyer's broom

Gratiola officinalis—hedge hyssop

Nicotiana tabacum—tobacco

Pinus—all kinds of pine

Raphanus sativus—black radish

Smilax utilis—sarsaparilla

Sinapis—all varieties of mustard

Sun

The Sun rules over: all life, as we know it. The Sun provides all of the other planets (including the Moon) with energy, which in turn they transform or modify, reflecting it back and thereby creating the impulses that influence the horoscope when they are perceived from the perspective of Earth. The Sun is our sense of self, willpower, total organizing ability (externally), self-integration (internally), total energy levels and vitality, and success.

The Sun corresponds to: the heart, and with it circulation (in relation to Mars and Jupiter); the distribution of heat in the body, as well as psychic energy (via the solar plexus); the spinal column; vision; thymus gland (near the heart); pituitary gland (with Mars and Saturn); and eyes: right in man, left in woman.

Diseases associated with the Sun are: diseases that affect the total health of the body, degrade the structure of the body, or are a result of birth defects or accidents.

Plants associated with the Sun include:

Anthemis nobilis—Roman chamomile

Calendula officinalis—marigold

Cinnamomum zeylanicum—cinnamon

Citrus bergamia—bergamot

Dictamnus albus—dittany

Euphrasia officinalis—eyebright

Helianthus annuus—sunflower

Hypericum perforatum—St. John's wort

Inula helenium—elecampane (sometimes Jupiter)

Matricaria chamomilla—German chamomile

Paeonia officinalis—peony

Rosmarinus officinalis—rosemary

Venus

Venus rules over: herbalism, spagyrics, talismanic and natural magic, arts, music, poetry, design, theater, harmony, proportion, integration and mediation of opposites into a whole, odors, perfumes, physical love, and celestial love (the Path of Devotion).

Venus corresponds to: the skin, complexion, muscles of the face, kidneys, perspiration, veins, parathyroid glands, tissue selection and formation, transformation and enrichment of substances within the body (or alchemically), internal sexual organs, and smell.

Diseases associated with Venus are: Venus, like Jupiter, does not promote disease but through its configuration with other planets can affect diseases, mainly of the skin, uterus, sexual organs, and kidneys, as well as, like Jupiter, diseases of immoderation and excess.

Plants associated with Venus include:

Achillea millefolium—yarrow

Alchemilla vulgaris—lady's mantle

Althaea officinalis—marshmallow

Cynara scolymus—artichoke

Fragaria vesca—wild strawberry

Leonurus cardiaca—motherwort

Persica vulgaris—peach

Pyrus communis—pear

Rosa damascena—rose

Rubus fructicosus—blackberry

Senecio jacobaea—tansy ragwort

Verbena officinalis—vervain

Mercury

Mercury rules over communications and commerce, initiation into the Mysteries, alchemy, Qabala, astrology, all forms of magic, writing, transmission of information, the nerves, skills involving manipulations and dexterity, mental skills, and the speedy distribution of energy.

Mercury corresponds to: the nerves, speech, hearing, the arms (fingers), the feet (toes), the brain (with the Moon), coordination between thoughts and speech or actions, the throat and thyroid, the pons in the brain (links the Sun [cerebrum] and Moon [cerebellum] aspects of the brain), spinal fluids, nerve sheaths, fluids related to the brain and nervous system, and in some instances the lungs (along with Jupiter).

Diseases associated with Mercury are: mental disorders, stuttering, and nerve disorders and breakdown, as well as respiration (under stress), metabolism, and metabolic disorders reflected in the thyroid.

Plants associated with Mercury include:

Acacia—all varieties of acacia

Anethum graveolens—dill

Apium graveolens—celery

Calamintha arvensis—mint, calamint

Carum carvi—caraway

Foeniculum vulgare—fennel

Marrubium vulgare—horehound

Mercurialis annua—(annual) mercury (and *perenis*, or perennial)

Pastinaca sativa—parsnip

Petroselinum hortense—parsley

Solanum dulcamara—bittersweet

Tussilago farfara—coltsfoot

Moon

The Moon rules over: water, growth, agriculture (with Saturn), fertility, conception, emotions, instincts and unconscious responses, psychic phenomena, family (mother), collective consciousness, rhythm and cycles, and genetic and cultural heritage.

The Moon corresponds to: the brain, memory (with Saturn), the breasts, the womb, the ovaries, menstruation, the stomach (with Jupiter) and esophagus, and all body fluids, including salivation, urination, and lactation.

Diseases associated with the Moon are: disruptions in any of the organs it rules, including dry breasts, infertility, and any glandular secretions (in conjunction with their specific planetary ruler), as well as the eyes: left in man, right in woman.

Plants associated with the Moon include:

Brassica—all varieties of cabbage

Cucurbita pepo—pumpkin gourd

Curcuma longa—turmeric

Hieracium pilosella—mouse-ear hawkweed

Hyssop officinalis—hyssop

Lenticula palustris—duckweed

Lilium album—white lily

Myristica fragrans—nutmeg

Nasturtium officinale—watercress

Stellaria media—chickweed

Veronica officinalis—speedwell

Vinca minor—periwinkle, myrtle (sometimes Saturn)

For a very thorough listing of plants, their Latin names, and their planetary correspondences, see *The Practical Handbook of Plant Alchemy*, by Manfred Junius. For a comprehensive listing of plants, their Latin names, their planetary and zodiacal correspondences, and cross-name listings for common names, see *The Master Book of Herbalism*, by Paul Beyerl. Additional suggested reading includes *A Modern Herbal*, by Mrs. M. Grieve, and *Culpeper's Medicine: A Practice of Western Holistic Medicine*, by Graeme Tobyn.

KEY POINTS

- Health is the body's natural state of being.

- Health must be sought not for itself, but as a means to continue our spiritual development and to aid others.

- If one is not a medical professional or under the care of one, diagnosing and treating with spagyric and alchemical products requires extensive experience. As such, we should only treat ourselves and not others if we do not possess the proper professional training. The practice of medicine is regulated by law in most countries.

- The body relies on mineral salts to maintain health.

- Homeopathy uses twelve of these salts in the creation of cell salts.

- Cell salts can also be used in the creation of spagyric products for restoring health.

- Mineral salts are found in the calcined salts of spagyric products and are an important part of the products' healing capacity, in part based on their astrological correspondences.

- Alchemical theory states that every person is born deficient in several cell salts. The degree of deficiency is a result of the length of fetal gestation in the womb. Since nobody develops for twelve months, nobody can be fully sufficient in all twelve salts.

- Plant salts, when calcined, will appear in one of seven crystalline formations. These formations correspond to the planets and the spheres on the Tree of Life in Qabala.

- Each planet affects several areas and functions of our psychic, physical, and mental health. Through correspondences, we can find the right plant and planetary ruler to create a tincture for sustaining health and well-being.

GENERAL ASSIGNMENTS FOR CHAPTER SEVEN

1. Make an Elixir from fresh rainwater and cell salts.

2. Review your notes and see how you can improve on the calcination of your salts.

MEDITATION PRACTICES FOR CHAPTER SEVEN

1. Using planetary hours, meditate on each of the crystalline structures presented. Do this for several weeks. Note the results of your meditations in your notebook.

2. Meditate on the nature of planetary correspondences. Starting on Saturday, sit with some horsetail (fresh or dried), or some other plant under the rulership of Saturn, and visualize yourself inside the plant's structure. What does it feel like to be horsetail? If possible, locate the position of Saturn in an ephemeris and face in its direction. Repeat this for each planet of each day, using the appropriate herb.

eight

RITUAL USE OF SPAGYRIC PRODUCTS

INNER TOOLS OF ALCHEMY

It was previously noted and stressed that for alchemy to be alchemy and not just an odd school of chemistry, the inner aspect must be consciously cultivated, maintained, and strengthened. Despite its inability to explain how the phenomenon works, modern science

CHAPTER OVERVIEW
- *Three Inner Tools of the Aspiring Alchemist*
- *Simple Consecration of Tincture as Talismans*
- *Holy Blood, Holy Grail— Fixing the Stone*

has demonstrated repeatedly in the laboratory that the attitude, the very *intention*, of the operator involved affects the outcome of various experiments in the field of particle physics. In *The Holographic Universe*, Michael Talbot described decades of research into the mind-brain-body connection and coupled it with cutting-edge research in physics. As mentioned in chapter 5, Dr. Bernard Grad at McGill University demonstrated the reality of the interconnectedness of the universe and the impact of emotions and focused thoughts on matter with some salt water, seeds, and potting soil.

From shamanic practices in Siberia to the Egyptian temples, right up to the current day, there has always been a belief in the flexibility of the universe and a belief that with the proper attitude and knowledge, each of us could literally shape destiny. While this belief has been expressed in a variety of practices and traditions, three fundamental tools remain consistent across time and cultures: prayer, ritual, and meditation.

Often seen as separate items, these three tools in combination are the means whereby each of us can enter into heightened states of awareness, knowledge, and well-being. In combination, they are the psychic counterpart to the three essentials of alchemy: meditation is sulphur, or the essence of things; prayer is mercury, or the messenger, the conveyer of ideas and desires; ritual is salt, or the physical action, the connection to physical life and matter. In more practical terms, we can say that in meditation we still our mind to experience a single idea, concept, or emotion or to be open to the influx of knowledge or psychic visions. In prayer, we verbally express our heartfelt desire. This desire can range from material wants and needs to the sublime desire to experience consciousness of the cosmos. In this regard, prayer shares many similarities with auto-suggestion, only the underlying principle is that our words are not limited to our own subconscious but rather are mediated through the subconscious to the collective consciousness, the cosmos, God, or whatever it is that represents the supreme universal power to the petitioner. Ritual takes our desire and expresses it dramatically through an orchestrated use of symbolism, color, sound, rhythm, and scent.

Throughout this book, a variety of meditations have been given to help aspiring alchemists focus their thoughts on a specific idea with the intention of deriving a personally meaningful experience—an experience that will assist them inwardly as well as in their laboratory work.

Ora et Labora

To fully understand prayer, we need to examine it in relationship to the uniquely alchemical phrase "Ora et labora," or "Prayer and work," from which we get the modern term *laboratory*. Each alchemical session in which you handle products, operate with materials, review notes from experiments, or study alchemical literature should open with a period of prayer. Prayer was well understood by the alchemists of the past, and it formed the basis for their inner work. Unfortunately, prayer has become an almost lost art and is now poorly understood, especially by modern students of esotericism. Much of this comes from an association of prayer with Jewish and Christian religious practice. Many Wiccans and Neopagans who have left these traditions retain a strong negative emotional connection to them that prevents them from really progressing on their new paths. This has resulted, in the last decade or so, in the belief that magic is a system of mechanics, actions, and ideas devoid of any moral or ethical frame-work. Morals and ethics are the stuff of "religion"; magic is seen as the stuff of "spiritual people" or "initiates on the path." This desire to separate morals and ethics from esoteric practices is unfortunate, as it is the single most important reason for failure in occult operations that exists. Lack of confidence might rank first, but all too often, lack of confidence comes from a feeling of unworthiness or an inner sense that success would not be handled well. In essence, failure is essentially a moral and ethical issue.

If we succeed, how will we act? How will we treat ourselves? How will we treat others? Occult practices are designed to demonstrate the interrelationship of energy, matter, and consciousness. To believe that this kind of universe could exist but that we as actors in it are the supreme judge of right and wrong is foolish. This does not mean that to be successful in esotericism you need to believe in a "Creator God" or God as a distinct personality, as these ideas are absent in many systems. It does mean, however, that each alchemist believes in a Godhead—a cosmic mind, or focal point of intelligence from which all things arise. This Godhead is difficult if not impossible to express, and for that reason, in Qabala it is referred to as the *Ain Soph Aur*, or "Limitless Light." This Limitless Light is also known as the "Three Veils of Negative Existence," called negative because the Godhead or fount of creation cannot be limited to anything, anyplace, or any-one, and therefore is limitless. It is active, conscious, and life-giving, and therefore is light.

Alchemists know that in relation to this awesome power and wis-dom, they are but mere shadows. They are humbled and in awe of the great mystery that creation is as well as their part in revealing, in their laboratories, the essence of all that is, was, or can be. To become greater than we are, we must remove the obstacles to our Becoming, our unfoldment. Through plant work, we can reduce and eliminate the psychic blockages that affect our physical and psychic bodies. But this is not enough if we simply fill them back up again with destructive thoughts, actions, and emotions. Yet of all the feelings that are destructive to our work, or to any work of spiritual progress, those feelings that will hold one back from experiencing the great height of spiritual Illumination, the worst is pride.

Pride is the worst of sins. When we say sin, we really mean the Hebrew word *khate*, from the root *khaw-taw*, which means "to err or miss the mark." As such, a sin is really an error, a mistake, something we did poorly through ignorance and misunderstanding. Pride is the worst form of ignorance, because it places one's self above all others. Even if justified because of professional or personal skill, pride separates us from others. Through it, we place ourselves on a pedestal and congratulate ourselves with false glory. Humility—sincere, genuine, and honest—is the hallmark of alchemists, humble because they know that they are the explorers of the vast territory of life, and not its owner or creator. Even as their consciousness merges into the Godhead, degree by degree, and their power and influence grows, genuine alchemists know that they are still but one aspect of the Divine Mind, and not the whole.

Unlike ritual, which requires the development of a superior state of mind, or meditation, which seeks to neutralize thoughts altogether, prayer is useful in establishing a humble and receptive attitude, in that typical prayer consists of a dialogue or conversation with our Inner Self, the Godhead within, and asks for assistance in the present undertaking.

The following prayer was left us by an anonymous German adept of the Great Art:

"O holy and hallowed Trinity, Thou undivided and triple Unity! Cause me to sink into the abyss of Thy limitless external Fire, for only in that Fire can the mortal nature of man be changed into humble dust, while the new body of the salt union lies in the light. Oh, melt me and transmute me in this Thy holy Fire, so that on the day at Thy command the fiery waters of the Holy Spirit draw me out from the dark dust, giving me new birth and making me alive with His breath. May I also be exalted through the humble humility of Thy Son, rising through His assistance out of the dust and ashes and changing into a pure spiritual body of rainbow colors like unto the transparent, crystal-like, paradisiacal gold, that my own nature may be redeemed and purified like the elements before me in these glasses and bottles. Diffuse me in the waters of life as though I were in the wine cellar of the eternal Solomon. Here the fire of Thy love will receive new fuel and will blaze forth so that no streams can extinguish it. Through the aid of this divine fire, may I in the end be found worthy to be called into the illumination of the righteous. May I then be sealed up with the light of the new world that I may also attain unto the immortality and glory where there shall be no more alternation of light and darkness. Amen."[1]

Alchemy flourished in the sixteenth century, a time that held "the magical notion that the mere pronunciation of words in a ritual manner could effect a change in the character of material objects." During this period of history, alchemy was a public event that could be experienced directly through the power of the Mass. Herein the cult of the Mass developed to such an extent that for many, it was believed that just seeing the host raised after its consecration was sufficient to receive its blessing. An occult practice even grew around the perceived power of the consecrated wine and wafer in which it is said that if a crystal ball is exposed to the consecration of the host, over time it will emit a red color. Magical practices such as this blur the line between folk traditions, high magic, and religion, and they were as common five hundred years ago as they are today.[2]

---

1 Manly P. Hall, *The Secret Teachings of All Ages* (New York: Tarcher, 2003). Also available online at www.sacred-texts.com/eso/sta.
2 Keith Thomas, *Religion and the Decline of Magic* (New York: Scribner's, 1971).

MEDITATION AND ALCHEMY

After having performed a few experiments, it should be clear that the entire alchemical process is a meditative one, that is, designed to bring the practitioner to the *medi*, or center, of his or her being. To facilitate this inward movement and outward expansion that meditation simultaneously brings, active and passive techniques can be utilized. Active forms involve visualization, concentration, and the creation of inner ideas, landscapes, and symbols in lifelike proportions. This is identical to practices found across the globe in a variety of esoteric systems, of which, in our modern age, Tibetan tantric practices seem to be most familiar. Qabalistic magic is based on these same three distinct and interrelated stages:

1. The student will meditate upon every detail of a particular image until he or she can visualize every detail clearly in the mind, even when performing other tasks.

2. This image will then be projected onto the material world, and with time can even be seen by other people, regardless of their psychic sensitivity.

3. With repeated visualization, the image becomes a material reality.

This process of repeated visualization and of reinforcing the desired goal to achieve not at some future date but to sense the unfoldment of the Philosopher's Stone in the present, forms the critical psychic basis for all alchemical work. To begin an alchemical operation without first seeing in your mind and in your heart the desired outcome is to stumble out of the gate. To undertake an alchemical operation that is not leading you toward or reinforcing your image of confecting the Stone of the Wise is to delay your progress. This forces students of the art to ask themselves, "Why am I doing this? What do I hope to gain?" In this manner, our motivation is always being checked to see if it is in alignment with our ultimate desire, thereby keeping us on track.

Passive meditation relies on the ability to hold the mind in check and to simply experience what is happening at a given moment in time with the least amount of psychic construction. Utilizing planetary hours is an example of passive meditation. Here, alchemists or Qabalists place themselves in a receptive state and allow the energies of the day and hour to fill them, inspire them, and reorganize their energies in a natural and harmonious fashion. To keep the mind open and receptive, a simple prayer or auto-suggestion is made that clearly gives the desired state of openness and receptivity; then, a single symbol may be used along with simple breathing techniques. The complex use of ritual, invocations, and even extensive prayers is eschewed, and instead the alchemist and his or her product becomes a sponge, absorbing the energies of the hour clearly, cleanly, and directly, with minimal mental filtering on the alchemist's part.

Technique for Passive Meditation

Prepare your meditation area, or *oratory* as it is called in several traditions (literally "place of prayer"), in the following manner:

1. Cover your altar, or the table you are using as an altar, with a black cloth. The cloth should preferably have a white border, but a simple piece of black cloth, large scarf, or even an unfolded handkerchief will do. Black is used because it is the color of Saturn and of Earth, both of which are concerned with "earthing" or "fixing" energy.

2. Place on top of the black cloth a drawing of the polygon and polygram combined that are appropriate for the planet that rules the herb that the tincture has been created from. For example, if the plant is ruled by Mars, a pentagon with a pentagram (five-pointed star) drawn inside of it—connecting all of the pentagon's points—would be used. Draw the planetary symbol in the center of the two symbols. This you can draw with black ink on a white piece of paper or index card. If possible, use the planetary color and its complementary color for

added effect. However, don't delay your work if they are not available; just use what is available to you and experience the simplicity of the process.

3. Place one white candle on your altar. White is used because it represents the pure undifferentiated energy of the Infinite that we are opening ourselves to. Incense appropriate to the planet may be used but is not essential. Have a candle snuffer at hand to use; never blow out your candles, as it is considered "extinguishing the light" rather than transforming it by using a candle snuffer.

4. A few minutes before the planetary hour of sunrise on the day ruling the planet and the symbol you are meditating on, light your candle and incense, if you are using any. If possible, arrange your space so that you are facing geographical east when seated in your oratory and before your altar.

5. Sit and breathe slowly and deeply through your nose. Let your mind and body relax and, after a minute or two of such breathing, say a prayer such as the following to set the tone for your operation: "May the Light of the Infinite infuse my mind, body, and consciousness with the Quintessence of [planet's name] and aid in my Awakening and any who I may come in contact with."

6. Breathe slowly and deeply, focusing on your breath and the idea that you are opening up to the energies of the planetary hour. Do not focus on what these energies are, how they feel, or what they should be doing. Simply bathe yourself in their presence.

7. If you need to focus on something to keep your mind from wandering, start small. Begin with the planetary symbol in its appropriate color, or simply inhale and exhale the color of the energy of the day. You can imagine the more complex symbol on your altar, but do not stress yourself if it is too complex to visualize at the moment. The key here is to keep everything simple and let Nature do her work.

8. Stay like this for fifteen to thirty minutes or even the entire length of the hour if you desire. When done, extinguish your candle and offer a prayer of thanks for whatever you have received, knowing that your meditation has been successful.

9. Give a closing sign, such as the Sign of Silence, performed by placing the index finger of the right hand to your lips. Hold this for a moment, with the intention of banishing any unabsorbed energies. You may also substitute this sign with a small bell, clapping your hands loudly, or anything else that signals a clean and clear end to the session.

RITUAL CHARGING OF ALCHEMICAL PRODUCTS

To passively charge an alchemical product is to take advantage of Nature's cyclic forces. Its advantage lies in its simplicity. It can be done under just about any circumstances and by anyone regardless of level of experience. Its disadvantage is that it often requires two or three sessions (although more can be performed) to bring a product to its level of potential psychic fullness. It is advisable to become familiar with this process, because in subtle but profound ways, the alchemist is also changed—changes that the more active methods do not always impart. This is partially because active methods of charging products, talismans, or ritual objects require that a certain degree of stress in the psychic environment be created. Once created, this stress must be released (without discharging the products it was imparted to). Nature always seeks balance, and if the energies invoked are not properly banished from the work area, or even the psyche of the operator, unpleasant experiences may result.[3]

Now, it is critical to clearly understand what we mean by invoking and banishing of energies. Invoking is analogous to taking a dry sponge and dropping it into a bucket of water so that it can be used.

---

3 *Tantra Unveiled: Seducing the Forces of Matter & Spirit*, by Pandit Rajmani Tigunait, Ph.D., is a brief overview of Indian tantric practices similar to those methods described here. Experienced students may find some of the similarities, as well as differences, of interest.

Banishing is taking the bucket of water and disposing of it after the sponge has been filled to its capacity. We do not seek to wring the water out of the sponge or to dry it out when we banish. That is why once charged, talismans or alchemical products are either consumed immediately, as in the Mass, or placed in a protective container, such as in a box or plastic bag or wrapped in nonconductive fabric.

Passive Charging

Prepare your ritual area in the following manner:

1. Cover your altar, or the table you are using as an altar, with a black cloth. The cloth should preferably have a white border, but a simple piece of black cloth, large scarf, or even an unfolded handkerchief will do. Black is used because it is the color of Saturn and of Earth, both of which are concerned with "earthing" or "fixing" energy.

2. Place on top of the black cloth a drawing of the polygon and polygram combined that are appropriate for the planet that rules the herb that the tincture has been created from. For example, if the plant is ruled by Mars, a pentagon with a pentagram (five-pointed star) drawn inside of it—connecting all of the pentagon's points—would be used. Draw the planetary symbol in the center of the two symbols. This you can draw with black ink on a white piece of paper or index card. If possible, use the planetary color and its complementary color for added effect. However, don't delay your work if they are not available; just use what is available to you and experience the simplicity of the process.

3. Place one white candle on your altar. White is used because it represents the pure undifferentiated energy of the Infinite that we are opening ourselves to. Incense appropriate to the planet may be used but is not essential. Have a candle snuffer at hand to use; never blow out your candles, as it is considered "extinguishing the light" rather than transforming it by using a candle snuffer.

4. A few minutes before the planetary hour of sunrise on the day ruling the tincture's planet, light your candle and place the tincture on top of the planetary symbol in the center of the card you have prepared. Be sure that the bottle is uncapped. If possible, arrange your space so that you are facing geographical east when seated in your oratory and before your altar.

5. Sit and breathe slowly and deeply through your nose. Let your mind and body relax and, after a minute or two of such breathing, say a prayer such as the following to set the tone for your operation: "May the Light of the Infinite infuse my mind, body, consciousness, and this tincture with the Quintessence of [planet's name] and aid in my Awakening and any who may come in contact with it."

6. Breathe slowly and deeply, focusing on your breath and the idea that you are opening up to the energies of the planetary hour. Do not focus on what these energies are, how they feel, or what they should be doing. Simply bathe yourself in their presence.

7. If you need to focus on something to keep your mind from wandering, start small. Begin with the planetary symbol in its appropriate color, or simply inhale and exhale the color of the energy of the day. You can imagine the more complex symbol on your altar, but do not stress yourself if it is too complex to visualize at the moment. The key here is to keep everything simple and let Nature do her work.

8. Stay like this for fifteen to thirty minutes or even the entire length of the hour if you desire. When done, recap your tincture, extinguish the candle, and offer a prayer of thanks for whatever you have received, knowing that the tincture has been charged.

9. Give a closing sign, such as the Sign of Silence, performed by placing the index finger of the right hand to your lips. Hold this for a moment, with the intention of banishing any unabsorbed energies. You may also substitute this sign with a small bell,

clapping your hands loudly, or anything else that signals a clean and clear end to the session.

A tincture can be charged in this manner as often as you like. It is not necessary to take lunar cycles into account when charging in this manner, because we are using planetary hours to compensate. However, taking advantage of lunar cycles will only enhance the operation. With experience, students are able to sense the arrival of the planetary hour as well as reduce the number of tools used in the charging. Over time, the geometric figures can be eliminated, as well as the candle and black covering. While there are distinct psychological advantages to using these tools repeatedly in order to induce the proper receptive state of mind, it will be possible in a pinch to charge a tincture simple by formulating a prayer, remaining passive at the proper hour, and leaving the tincture uncapped for several minutes.

Active Charging

Active charging of products differs from passive charging more in form than in substance. Both methods are designed to increase the amount of energy a product contains and is therefore available to the alchemist (or whoever uses the product) when he or she decides to use it. Methods can range from very elaborate personalized rituals involving the pentagram and hexagram, or the elaborate alchemical ritual given in the Hermetic Order of the Golden Dawn's Z-2 document, to simple consecrations and blessings.[4] Two simple forms of active charging are detailed here, and more elaborate methods of charging can be found in works dealing with talismans.

---

4 For a description of the pentagram and hexagram rituals, the Z-2 document, and additional information on geometric figures and talismans, see: Israel Regardie, *The Golden Dawn* (St. Paul, MN: Llewellyn Publications, 1989).

Simple Active Charging

While planetary hours are being used in this method of active charging, it is more important to take lunar cycles into account than in the passive method previously described. Preferably, you should perform operations of this nature only when the Moon is waxing, that is, during the period between the New Moon and Full Moon. Avoid charging during the waning Moon unless there is the distinct need for dense, heavy, material force. In this case, it is possible to begin the operation during the New Moon and charge the product repeatedly for the entire lunar month of four weeks, or even a forty-two-day period. A charging of this length can be done every day for the entire period, or just on the planetary hour after sunrise on the day of the ruling planet.

Equipment Needed

You will need all of the tools listed in the directions for passive charging above; in addition, it is important that you have an understanding of the qualities represented by the planet involved and that you have available as much symbolic paraphernalia related to the planet and the function of the tincture as you can.

Technique for Active Charging

1. Prepare your oratory prior to the actual ritual. It is preferable that you establish the altar so that you will be facing the geographical direction of the planet whose forces you are attuning to, or, as a second choice, facing geographical east. However, the ritual can proceed if neither of these positions is known. Begin the ritual a few minutes after sunrise on the day ruling the planet corresponding to the tincture.

2. Relax, preparing yourself for the work ahead.

3. Stand, facing front or east, extend your right hand, and trace a brilliant bluish white circle about your work area. This circle should be imagined to be about nine feet in diameter and, when completed, form a brilliant translucent sphere about

the area in which it is imagined. Take your time with this and imagine it strongly.

4. Recite aloud your opening prayer or petition. Prayers said out loud rather than whispered or given silently have a greater emotional impact and therefore greater power. Here is an example: "Great Nothingness from which All has come, open my heart, mind, and body to Nature's powers of the day and hour; and with her aid, in the light of day lift up my soul like the morning sun to shed Light and Life upon all that it touches. In the Name and the Power of the Great Work, Amen!"

5. Imagine a brilliant sphere of white light forming before you, about a foot or so above your head. Imagine it growing bright, dense, and shining in color. Lift up your arms so that the sphere appears to be floating between your hands.

6. Imagine the sphere changing from brilliant white to the color of the planet of the day. Imagine that it is outlined by highlights of the planet's complementary color. Visualize the symbol of the planet of the day in the center of the sphere, this too in its complementary color.

7. Breathe deeply, imagining your body filled with brilliant energy. This can be bluish white or the color of the day. Fill yourself with this energy, and as you exhale, see it moving out of your hands into the sphere and imagine the sphere responding to this increase in energy. Focus a strong emotional theme to the energy. Imagine the actual outcome that you desire the tincture to bring as being played out inside the sphere, as if it were a miniature video screen.

8. As you slowly lower your hands, imagine the sphere moving down with them, until it is hovering over your tincture. Pause and strengthen your image if needed.

9. Imagine the sphere around the tincture, and charge it for several breaths.

10. Imagine the sphere entering into the bottle and being completely absorbed into the tincture.

11. Cap the bottle.

12. Sit and relax for a few moments.

13. Rise. Face east. Recite your closing prayer: "Great Nothingness from which All has come, thank you for the presence of Nature's powers on this day and hour, and for her aid, that in the light of day this part of my Becoming has been accomplished. In the Name and the Power of the Great Work, Amen!"

14. Trace counterclockwise a circle, and as you do, imagine the sphere collapsing and opening up. Pause when you complete your circle.

15. Give the Sign of Silence or some other suitable closing gesture. Firmly feel the energies invoked released from the area of working, and feel everything return to normal.

Active and Passive Methods: A Comparison and Contrast

The advantages and disadvantages to the methods of active and passive charging of an Elixir or talisman are straightforward and simple. Passive charging, like passive meditation, allows the natural energies of the moment to permeate the consciousness of the one meditating, or fill the energetic matrix of the object by simply "getting out of the way" and letting Nature do what she does best. This is a wonderful method for those who have little or no experience in meditation or in charging of products, and it can be done with little or no equipment. Its chief disadvantages are that the method must be done several times to get the maximum charge. In passive meditation, the chief disadvantage lies in the one meditating. The technique is so simple that students often feel as though they need to be doing something for it to work, and thereby they keep their minds agitated rather than observing and experiencing the energies and images that arise in the moment. Often, they simply convince themselves that the method is too simple and therefore cannot work. This same doubt can enter into the charging process as well, thereby impacting the chances of success by polluting the psychic environment of the process. A large part of this need for the mind to be active—jumping from idea to idea—is a result of cultural degradation via popular media and video games, coupled with a limited number of magical sources whose traditions are overlaid with excessive Masonic and psuedo-Masonic stylization in their rituals. Combined, these two sources have created a generation of students that finds it difficult to focus the mind on a single point, or to be mentally receptive without being manipulated by external stimulation at the same time. Developing the ability to meditate passively is the single most important key to psychic development and receptivity. It is a significant step in the direction of mental self-mastery.

Active meditation and charging have the chief benefit of being able to work on a specific topic during a sitting and being able to charge an Elixir or talisman in a single operation. Their chief drawback is twofold: one, that if a period of relaxation and release do not follow, a sense of mental agitation pervades the session and ruins the work, and two, that the operator can become overly involved and, while having success, color it too much with his or her own pathology.

The proper balance of active and passive phases must be struck for either method to work effectively. For passive techniques, the key is in the initial setup and then letting Nature take over while being an alert but passive observer. For the active methods, the key is in staying single-mindedly focused on the moment and then, when the operation is complete, completely disengaging from it emotionally and mentally and returning to day-to-day consciousness.

HOLY BLOOD, HOLY GRAIL

In ancient times, when a detailed understanding of genetics was not available, the idea of qualities being passed on from generation to generation was seen in the breeding practices of farm animals and humans. To have "good blood" or be from a "blue blood" family was seen as desirable, whereas "weak blood" was used to describe social and physical traits that were seen as undesirable. This in part was a holdover from earlier practices of the caste system, such as was upheld in India until the mid-twentieth century and is still practiced in remote rural areas there. In recent years, this idea of royal blood or genetically enhanced qualities being passed on as a result of spiritual practices is found in the belief that Jesus Christ married Mary Magdalene and their children went on to be the royal heads of Europe, and France in particular. While this is a difficult and tricky historical topic to enter into, each of us can experiment to some degree with the idea that our blood, or personal fixed mercury (salt and mercury combined), is in some way affected by what we do and in turn affects the work. Generally, tests involving an alchemist's blood are for acts of transmutation and, as such, are dangerous, in that they involve metallic mercury. However, tests involving the fixing, or making permanent, of an energetic quality brought on by a plant tincture can be undertaken without any harm.

In general, the effects of plant products peak and begin to wear off after one week. For this reason, they must continually be used or a means of fixing their effects must be found. Fixing can be done in one of two ways: either with mineral salts of gold, such as were listed in the previous chapter, or with a homeopathic dilution of one's own blood. Clearly, for health and ethical reasons, once a tincture is fixed with blood, even a diluted drop, it can only be used by its creator and not shared with anyone else. Tinctures fixed with gold salts, however, can be shared.

The process is simple:

1. Prick your finger to obtain a drop of blood. Squeeze off the first two or three drops and dispose of them properly. Take the third or fourth drop and place it in a small vial containing ten drops of distilled water.

2. Shake vigorously ten times to mix the two fluids.

3. Take one drop of this fluid and mix it with ten drops of distilled water. Shake ten times.

4. Repeat this dilution again, at one drop of blood tincture to distilled water.

5. Finally, take one drop of this final dilution and place it in the tincture you wish to fix.

6. Dispose of the remaining fluids properly.

The advantage to this process is that it can be done anywhere with no special equipment; the disadvantage, of course, is that it makes your tincture available only to yourself. Now, it is important to note that fixing the effects of the tincture does not mean that you should stop ingesting your products, only that it enhances the accumulative quality of them rather than allowing it to dissipate over time. This dissipation or accumulation is also impacted by your spiritual practices and daily habits, as well as your health and hygiene.

KEY POINTS

- The universe is increasingly being viewed as a sort of "hologram" in which we individually and collectively affect the outcome.

- Emotions affect living organisms and even inanimate matter.

- Scientific research at McGill University demonstrated the effect of emotions on water and their ability to change the growing patterns of seeds.

- Prayer, meditation, and ritual are just as important in alchemy as they are in Qabala and other systems of spirituality.

- There are two methods of meditation and two techniques for charging an Elixir or talisman: passive and active.

- The Christian Mass is considered in its esoteric form to be one of the greatest and simplest examples of operative alchemy and talismanic magic.

- During the Middle Ages and the Renaissance, cults of the Mass developed in which there developed among the folk traditions a belief in the profound healing and spiritual powers found in merely witnessing the Mass.

GENERAL ASSIGNMENTS FOR CHAPTER EIGHT

1. If you have not done so already, take the time to draw the geometric figures suggested. Draw them in black and white, and later draw them in their complementary colors.

2. Read several articles in the *Encyclopedia of Religion*, or in other available reference sources, on the following topics: sympathetic magic, talismans, natural magic, the Mass, and sacred geometry.

MEDITATION PRACTICES FOR CHAPTER EIGHT

1. Undertake the practice of passive and active meditation as detailed in this chapter. You may alternate between the methods, with active in the morning and passive in the evening (or vice versa), if you like.

2. Utilize a short prayer or petition before one of your sessions. Notice if it makes any difference in your experience.

3. Practice short periods of prayer often across the day, even if just for a minute or two. This can be a short, simple affirmation coupled with a single clear symbol or image that you use throughout the day. Try to do this every hour if possible.

nine

THE RED AND WHITE STONES OF ALCHEMY

THE STONES OF THE ROYAL ART

Alchemy is often called "the Royal Art" and is considered to be the pinnacle of Hermetic practices. Its goal is to perfect the human personality through a series of chemical and metallurgical opera-

tions, which, if successfully completed, are seen as a material demonstration of an achieved interior state. Like the *siddhas* of yoga or the *charismen* of the New Testament, various abilities at transmutation become available to adepts as they climb the Hermetic ladder. Among the best known of these abilities are the power to transmute one metal or mineral into another; the power to cure disease through the creation of a universal medicine, or *panacea*; and the ability to live a long life, nearing immortality by human standards, through creation of the *Elixir Vitae*.

Just as a talisman of paper, metal, or stone binds a certain amount of planetary energy to it for a specific purpose, the alchemical Elixir of Life is the etheric life force in a liquid state of matter. The alchemical Stone of the Wise (or Red Stone) is the etheric life force in a solid state of matter. *Each is the maximum amount of energy possible stored in a minimum quantity of liquid or solid matter.* The Elixir of Life is related to other spiritual liquids as well, including the *homa* of

Zoroastrianism, *soma* of the Vedas, *ambrosia* of the Greeks, and *cinnabar* in Taoist alchemy.

Alchemy traditionally has shown itself to pose three expressions or aspects: metallurgical-chemical, physiological-homeopathic, and ethical-spiritual. The language of medieval and Renaissance spiritual alchemy in Germany demonstrates this progression in the injunction that each "philosopher" is to be transformed from a dead stone into a living Philosophical Stone. By making himself into a "living Stone," each alchemist becomes the *lapis philosopher* ("Stone of the Wise"), which in turn can act in the world as a *panacea* (Greek for "all-healing") on others. This *plusquamperfectum*, or perfection, exists on all planes of matter and consciousness. It heals bodily ills as well as moral and ethical ills and restores the user to a state of spiritual grace, if not outright purity.

Each alchemist thereby becomes a focal point of energy, a small sun in the universe of humanity, whereby simply being physically close to him or her can allow a certain change in consciousness and physical health. The alchemist radiates life just as the sun radiates light—and from light, life and consciousness arise. This is critical, for at this point, the alchemist no longer administers healing products or medicines, but instead, *he or she is the healing medicine.* The very presence of the alchemist heals.

We have seen in earlier experiments that the relationship between energy, matter, and consciousness form a triad that exists to varying degrees in everything. The spectrum of energy and matter exists in its own domain, and from its constant operations, consciousness arises. After a period of time, consciousness gives way to self-consciousness, and its relationship with matter and energy move from the chaotic and unpredictable to the orderly and predictable. It is through this ability to apply consciousness to the relationship of matter and energy that practical occultism is possible. If it were not so, the use of both active imagination in magical ritual and material experiments in alchemy to create change in the material world, via the principle of "As above, so below," would be self-delusion.

The four elements form the etheric-material base that gives rise to the three essentials. Of the elements, fire plays the most significant part, for "etheric fire" (i.e., energy) gives rise to self-consciousness; it is the foundational energy for human consciousness as well as the means of transforming matter from raw to refined states:

> The fire principle plays a predominant part in many alchemical treatises, for it is the soul of the Microcosm. The elemental atoms of this fire, certain alchemists tell us, pervade the universe in the form of currents; these produce light when they intersect in the heavens, and gold when they meet beneath the ground. Light and gold are sometimes considered to be fire in its concrete state: to "materialize" this gold, which is sown profusely throughout the world, one need only condense widely scattered atoms. Properly speaking, gold is not a metal—gold is light.[1]

The colors black, white, and red play important parts in the stages of material transformation.

Black, or negrado, is death.

White, or albus, is calcination, the purification of the body.

Red, or rubeo, is the perfection of the reunited body and consciousness (salt and sulphur).

Yellow is sometimes mentioned as an intermediary stage between the white and red stages and represents perfect fecundation.

What makes alchemy different from many other occult arts is hinted at in the color red. Red is the reuniting of the consciousness and the body. It is enlightenment in the world, and not escape from it. The Red Stone permeates all creation and anchors the energies of the cosmos into the physical life.

It may be coincidence that with these four colors we have the four colors of Tibetan Buddhism as well. However, it is important to know that some old schools of Buddhism place their doctrinal origins in

---

1 M. Caron and S. Hutin, *The Alchemists*, trans. Helen R. Lane (New York: Grove Press, Inc., 1961), 163–164.

Egypt. The Bon tradition, the oldest of the Tibetan religions and indigenous to that land prior to the arrival of Buddhism, claims three places of influence for its doctrines and practices, one being modern Persia.[2]

Persia was invaded by the Aryan people (hence the modern name Iran), who came from the Caucasus Mountains, the area now known to be the home of Sanskrit, "the mother of all languages," giving some physical connection to these ancient traditions. There is also evidence that people from the Caucasus may be the source for Egypt's mystery teachings on some level. Evidence also suggests that this region of the world may have been home to the primordial tradition sought by so many students of esotericism.

The colors can be used to designate a degree of perfection of a particular alchemical product, with black referring to something in its "natural" state, white being a medicine that strongly affects the body and etheric forces, and red being a product that affects primarily the consciousness of the recipient but also, as a result, emotional, etheric, and physical well-being. These two Elixirs or Stones are known as the White Elixir or Stone and the Red Elixir or Stone. This gives us two levels of products: one mainly physical, and one aimed at the spiritual. There is a third product, little spoken of, called the *Fire Stone*, which affects the spiritual on a highly transcendental level. Little is known or written of this Stone, and it may refer to a perfection on the plane of consciousness related to Saturn (Binah), just as the Red and the White refer to the Sun (Tiphareth) and the Moon (Yesod) respectively.

An excerpt from a 1928 Rosicrucian manuscript on alchemy by Francis Mayer, a well-known student of Hermetic philosophy, states:

> As the colors indicate, the process is the same as followed in the Work for the Stone, where first the black developed and out of it in succession the white and the red, as the work progresses through the elemental, the sidereal [astral] and the mental worlds. The elixir

---

2 Tenzin Wangyal Rinpoche, *Healing with Form, Energy and Light* (Ithaca, NY: Snow Lion Publications, 2002), xix.

used for medical purposes and to rejuvenate the body is the second elixir, white or red, both of them obtained by circulations and imbibitions. White and Red, like moon and sun, are essentially the same in alchemy as substances, except the lunar white is less fiery, is cooler and less intensive, more moderated as is the red or solar elixir, the potable gold. The circulations are made through the seven so-called planets and imbibed substance is what is known as higher or zodiacal element, in plain language, aether [vital life energy], reaching us through the constellations.

Now in alchemy, the zodiac and the planets are considered as located in the organism of man, including the auric bodies, the vital [etheric], sidereal [astral], even the solar [mental] bodies. In consequence of this duplicity, i.e., physical and hyper-physical, of our organism complicated by the fact that it functions on four planes, the ancients were reticent and left it to the initiator to reveal the exact locations of stars and planets in the body, because it could be understood by the practitioner only, who is familiar with hyper-physical organisms and planes of consciousness. Moreover, they knew by experience that unskilled handling of this delicate and complicated machinery may cause transitory or even permanent malfunctional disorders.

And further on:

So while it is still difficult to find the exact actual locations, it has become an open secret that the planets and the zodiac of the sun as well as of the moon [psychic centers] are centered in or around the brain, the spine, the glands and the diverse plexus. Also that these organs are in more or less constant and intense intercommunication with the circumambient aether. Consequently, the seven circulations and following imbibitions by which the white and red elixirs are produced, mean in plain English but circulations of our vital energy, our fixed power, through different plexus and glands, also brain and spine, as well as the reinforcing of this energy by imbibitions from the circumambient aether, our volatile mercury, which by the operation is drawn in, becomes assimilated, coagulated and fixed in our organism.

The indicated fact that the sun, moon, and mercury have to be united, informs the alchemist, that, in the operation, the solar plexus as governor of all the other plexus, and the gonads (the testicles or the ovaries according to the sex of the operator) as governor of the other glands, also the glands in the brain are the main factors. Thus, these circulations energize through the solar plexus, the whole sympathetic nervous system, while the glands energized stimulate the production of the hormones, governors of the vegetative part of our life and to a certain extent of our emotional life too. It is not difficult to comprehend that such stimulations performed regularly and in accordance with the methods of Tradition could have curative effects, and when continued systematically were able to keep body and mind vigorous, even to rejuvenate it and prolong life to its natural limits. For our old alchemists were less optimistic than some modern doctors who believe that life in the flesh can be extended indefinitely.

As is well known, the alchemist and the *magus* had to observe certain self-discipline before they started operations. This consisted of the purification of body and mind, moderation in eating, strict sobriety, abstinence from sexual relations, also frequent meditations and prayers, during at least a whole week before commencing the circulations and imbibitions. The intention of this discipline is obvious. They desired to store up or conserve by saving the vital and especially the generative energy, and to imbue the other organs with it, also to make themselves fit, by purification of body and mind, to attract the aether and to be able to bear the more rapid and intenser vibrations of the higher vitality. The special esoteric prayers were to prepare the inner mind for the expected higher states of consciousness and to attract the primordial aether. Modern medical science [*Author's note:* "Modern" as of the 1920s] which experiments with good results chiefly with the endocrine glands and the gonads to cure and rejuvenate men, could safely endorse these preparations.

But while the operations mentioned did their work on the alchemist himself, in order to have the elixir ready at hand or to administer it to others, it was necessary to embody it into to some substance which could be handled as any other medicine. Paracelsus and Bulwer Lytton indicate sufficiently how this was done: Certain plants, mentioned only as "Simples," have been gathered, their quintessence taken out in liquid or pulverized form, the curative properties of which were then enhanced by projecting on it, and incorporating into it, the tincture, the reinforced and enobled vital energy of the alchemist. . . . [Matter] gathered [his] simples . . . and out of these made only two groups of medicaments, one for the lymphs and the other for the blood, for according to [alchemical] theory, all diseases originating in the patient are caused by corruptions of one or the other of these fluids. Considering the close relationship between the lymph and the blood as well as their respective colors, the analogy between these two groups of medicaments and the white and red elixir impress itself on the mind. . . .

White and red elixirs, however, likewise their modern substitutes, are but the second elixir, curative and rejuvenating. But hardly anything is or was printed concerning the third elixir produced by fermentation, the spiritual and only complete elixir, which should rejuvenate man and make him immortal.[3]

The author of this manuscript refers to the solar plexus as the master of the other nerve plexi in the human body. In esoteric physiology, the solar plexus is critical because it acts as a tuning fork for the psychic body and distributes energy to the other plexi. The exact location of the solar plexus varies from system to system, with it often being located in the navel as well as near the heart. However, if we look at the function of the solar plexus, we can see that it is located in the area of the stomach. The solar plexus distributes energy—and can even store it—but it does not generate energy. That is left to the other centers. The ability to absorb and distribute energy is crucial from the occult point of view. The idea that the stomach can absorb and distribute energy can be found in Egyptian funeral texts and earlier shamanic legends and practices. Shamans were said to have a white phlegm in the stomach that was their power, and they could spit this out for their students to partake of in a sort of ritualistic cannibalism.

Perceptions of the energies as they are radiated from the solar plexus tend to be more emotional and physical in expression than when perceived from other psychic centers.

Paracelsus states that the Secret Fire (which he calls the *Archeus*, or Quintessence), also known as *cosmic energy* in modern terms, is equally distributed throughout the human body. The life energy (*Spiritus Vitae*) is derived from the Sun's energies as they interact with Earth (*Spiritus*

---

3 Francis Mayer, "The Ancient and Modern Elixirs of the Alchemists," *Mercury* (March and June 1928). Mayer was an important figure in the early years of the Societas Rosicruciania in America (SRIA), penning many articles for the organization's publication. Special thanks to Maria Babwahsingh, Imperatrix of the SRIA, for providing permission to quote the above material.

Mundi) and contains all cosmic influences. It is the cause by which the cosmic forces act upon the physical world and human body. The single most important aspect of the Secret Fire is that it is magnetic in nature and is not limited by the physical body but rather radiates within the cells of the body and around it, forming the human aura. Its predominant geometric characteristic is that it forms luminous spheres when it is concentrated.

In alchemy, there is one essence, the Hyle or Chaos of the alchemists, which divides into niter and salt, which in turn give rise to life and matter; but this is not completely true, as the division is not complete. There is no break between these two extremes of manifestation—one being pure active energy and the other being pure passive energy, or matter. The analogy of keys on a piano is more fitting, as continuity, repetition, and increase or decrease in octave is the Path of Nature.

Just as this apparent division—or more accurately, as we said, discrete concentrations of various levels of life energy—appears on the grand or cosmic level, we see its reflection in our solar system, with the Sun's energy providing both active and passive expressions to each of the planets and the Moon acting as the Sun's "shadow."

In the physical world we inhabit, this polarity is seen in the expression of the elements. In our bodies, it is seen as the two main psychic channels, one active, one passive, both supplied by the same energy, and the various points of concentration of this energy when the channels overlap—or the psychic centers. The process is repeated regardless of the realm, with all beings composed of various degrees of sulphur (consciousness), mercury (energy), and salt (matter).

Archaic occult systems, such as shamanism, and later developments, including Qabala, often used only three principal psychic centers, which correspond to the three critical areas of the body: head, heart, and stomach. On a physical level, life could not be sustained if one or more of these areas were seriously damaged. On a psychic level, they are seats of emotional power and energy. The *Sepher Yetzirah* assigns to them the three "mother" letters of the Hebrew alphabet: Shin, or fire, corresponds to the head; Aleph, or air, to the heart or chest; and Mem, or water, to the stomach. In alchemy, similar attributions are given: mercury to the head, sulphur to the heart, and salt to the stomach.

In individuals for whom the energies of matter (salt) dominate, concrete ideas will dominate, along with powerful passion and instinct. Violence and criminal activity will not disturb them, and they will have very little energy of self-conscious nature. In individuals for whom the energies of the mind (mercury) dominate, thought and abstraction will come quickly and easily, as well as an interest in esoteric and occult topics. In those whom the energies of Being (sulphur) dominate, religious (particularly devotional mysticism) and esoteric ideas will hold a powerful sway. They are broadly active, and they acquire wealth easily.

The purpose of the brain (mercury) is to act as a bridge, a tool, between self-consciousness (sulphur) and the body (salt). The energies of the body are needed and useful, but they must be purified. If they are destroyed, then consciousness cannot manifest. If they dominate, then consciousness is dramatically reduced. The actions of mercury (mind-brain) must be to constantly unite these two expressions of energy. These attributes are meant to demonstrate that the physical body, when in harmony with the mental and emotional qualities of consciousness, becomes a living Philosophical Stone. They also give us keys for our meditations when working with the ideas surrounding the three essentials. These essentials have specific areas of concentration; however, each psychic center has its own "essentials." For example, salt or matter is assigned to the stomach or navel. This means the psychic centers at and below the stomach are concerned with the material functions of the body. However, to carry this out, they also need energy (mercury) and specific intelligence or direction (sulphur).

In alchemy, hypnosis, and other occult practices, we often notice that the body is subordinate to the subconscious but that they are both identical in function. Our physical body synthesizes and produces a vast array of material substances from the food we give it.

When this is of high quality and in ample supply, we are able to be healthy, energetic, and in harmony with our psychic qualities as well. Our physical body has all that it needs to be transmuted into a "living Stone," and our consciousness will transmute with it into a miniature Hermes or true alchemist incarnate if properly directed.

In the same fashion, our subconscious creates for us a synthetic whole based upon the quality of "food" (emotions, images, and ideas) that we "feed" it. As long as we live, they are combined into a single body and state of consciousness. The main place where this digestion, assimilation, and distribution of psychic and physical energy takes place is in the stomach and its attendant organs. From the psychic point of view, this is the solar plexus and nerve ganglia associated with the physical aspects of its functioning.

> **Salt**—The body's salt is derived exclusively from the material world, from the food we eat and liquids we drink. The quality and quantity of food we eat directly impacts our physical health and well-being. The diaphragm controls reparation, and therefore the amount of energy the body takes in. Yet despite poor nutrition, the body is an efficient machine that is also able to extract life energy from the air we breathe.

> **Mercury**—The air we breathe supplies us with the necessary mercury, or life energy (Secret Fire), that animates our physical bodies. To acquire adequate mercury, it is essential to breathe deeply and fully. Schools of meditation use various forms of rhythmic breathing for this purpose, as well as to strengthen and purify the body (salt) so that it can be imbibed with more spiritual consciousness (sulphur). The planet Mercury rules the nervous system, respiration, and communication between the inner and outer consciousness.

> **Sulphur**—Our sulphur is our consciousness. Since our three essentials cannot be completely separated and recombined easily (astral projection and sleep being the exceptions), we must constantly watch our thoughts and feelings so that we generate

goodwill and seek to benefit others. Our body responds to the thoughts and feelings we hold. In this manner, the salt purifies our consciousness by giving tangible expression to our feelings. As we hold in our heart, so we are.

The three principles or essentials of mercury, sulphur, and salt must be understood in their macrocosmic and microcosmic interpretations for genuine alchemy (i.e., transmutating power) to be developed and expressed.

The key to success on the alchemical path is simple: be confident and focused in your work; be kind, generous, and helpful to others; be imperturbable in the face of confusion and chaos; and be humble by knowing that all alchemical work prepares us for Illumination, but only inner grace can give it.

THE ROLE OF SATURN IN ALCHEMY

"Saturn eats its young" is frequently heard in astrological circles and refers to the effects time has on all of creation. What is created will at some point become uncreated. What lives will die. Nothing in the material world is permanent. The entire Buddhist philosophy is based upon this simple truth. The Egyptians embraced death, knowing that it was forever their destiny as mortals. Yet even here we see an attempt to cheat death, be it through enlightenment or the rites of mummification. Jews and Christians in their own ways also seek to cheat death through the belief in the possibility, or even the guarantee, of physical resurrection of the dead.

According to Cornelius Agrippa, "In the human body there is a very small bone called *Luz* by the Hebrews, which is the size of a pea, and is incorruptible, also it is not capable of being damaged by fire, but always remains unhurt. According to Jewish tradition, when the dead are raised, our new bodies will sprout from it as plants do from seeds. . . . However, these powers cannot be fathomed by the mind, but have to be verified empirically."[4]

---

4 Henry Cornelius Agrippa of Nettesheim, *Three Books of Occult Philosophy*, ed. Donald Tyson (St. Paul, MN: Llewellyn Publications, 1993), chapter XX.

Other occult philosophers locate the Luz bone along the spine or in the skull at various locations. For our purposes, we will discuss the symbolism of the Luz from the perspective of Agrippa. Luz means "inward-curving," and it is easy to see how it can refer to the base of the spine.

If we take the modern zodiacal wheel and place Leo and Cancer at the Midheaven and Capricorn and Aquarius at the low Heaven, we can begin to see how the planets and astrological signs match and suggest planetary correspondences for the psychic centers. Now, this distinction is important. We are referring to psychic centers, not the psychic body of a physical organ or the planetary energy of a physical organ, but specifically to a point of contact between the physical and the psychic *in the etheric body* that transmits energy in the physical body.

Planet	Zodiac	Major Psychic Center	Element of the Zodiacal Sign	Ganglia/ Gland	Alternate Attribution for the Psychic Centers
Sun	Leo	☉	Fire (+)	Coronal/ Pineal	Sun (Active—Niter)
Moon	Cancer	☽	Water (–)	Frontal or Medulla Oblongata	Moon (Passive—Salt)
Mercury	Gemini Virgo	☿	Air (+) Earth (–)	Laryngeal	Spirit (Quintessence)
Venus	Taurus Libra	♀	Earth (–) Air (+)	Cardiac	Air
Mars	Aries Scorpio	♂	Fire (+) Water (–)	Epigastric	Fire
Jupiter	Sagittarius Pisces	♃	Fire (+) Water (–)	Prostatic	Water
Saturn	Capricorn Aquarius	♄	Earth (–) Air (+)	Sacral	Earth

This point of contact can be described in astrological, elemental, or planetary terms, and depending on your perspective, that is how they will be experienced. This multiplicity of seemingly contradictory correspondences for the various psychic centers can be easily resolved if each set of correspondences is looked at separately as an independent system. Second, you must consider the designations given to each center in terms of function. What is it that the psychic center is supposed to do within the system? This will help you to understand why certain symbolic relationships were established. This ability to focus and keep ideas in context is important. Similar qualities does not mean interchangeable. Correspondences means that things are alike or similar to each other but does not mean they are equal. "Equal" is a mathematical term that means "interchangeable." The relationships presented in psychic anatomy are complex and cannot be reduced to simple ideas of universality and interchangeability. Use psychic centers and their symbols as starting points of energy, not as endpoints. With over seven hundred psychic functions in the human body, there will always be areas of disagreement between systems and models, as these are but humanity's crude attempt to put into concrete language, set in time and space, experiences that are synthetic, dynamic, and changing depending on an individual's degree of initiation, or personal integration.

> The varieties of the hermetico-alchemical symbolism in which, one way or the other, the Seven figure can be interpreted at the microcosmic level . . . to specific points of the body so rigorously followed in the Orient . . . are rarely encountered in hermeticism. We encounter the most explicit reference—conforming quite closely to the Hindu teaching in this matter—to the fourth illustration annexed to George Gichtel's *Theosophia practica*. In this illustration, the coronal, frontal, laryngeal, cardiac, lumbar, umbilical, and sacral regions are indicated by means of the hermetico-astrological ideograms of the planets affixed at points given in each of these regions.[5]

The order of correspondence given to the psychic centers relates directly to the path one is working. While centers are stimulated by the work, not all are opened in the same order or to the same degree in all Paths. Only at the very beginning of the work, when each being is in ignorance, and at the end, when each is Illumined, can they be said to

---

5 Julius Evola, *The Hermetic Tradition: Symbols and Teachings of the Royal Art* (Rochester, VT: Inner Traditions, 1995), 57.

be "equal." It is foolish, time wasting, and in some instances dangerous to interchange systems and correspondences as if they were parts of a child's toy.

KEY POINTS

- Alchemy has three aspects: chemical-metallurgical, physiological-macrobiotic, and spiritual-ethical.

- Transmutation, healing, and longevity are concrete expressions of inner states of consciousness.

- Interior purification and transmutation must occur prior to external transmutations.

- Light is the key to magic (and alchemy); light is life; matter is solidified light.

- Gold is the perfect expression of matter, and therefore light, in the material world.

- The endocrine, nervous, and circulatory (blood and lymph) systems are all stimulated and brought to higher levels of functioning by alchemical experiences.

- Fire is energy. Colors represent the stages of the work, or intensity of energy and degrees of perfection of the matter.

GENERAL ASSIGNMENTS FOR CHAPTER NINE

1. Review your experiments to date. Pay attention to how well you were able to handle the fire or energy aspect of the operations. Were you in a hurry? Did you push the fire up and down constantly to either speed up the experiment or prevent damage to the matter? Has your tolerance for heat, light, and work requiring patience increased since you began your alchemical work?

2. Obtain a general text on human anatomy and become familiar with the basic systems and functions of the human body.

3. Read a book on general astrology. Pay attention to the idea of cycles and character influences as a result of cosmic radiations.

MEDITATION PRACTICES FOR CHAPTER NINE

1. Imagine yourself as having completed the Great Work of alchemy, as being in possession of the Philosopher's Stone, the panacea to cure all ills, and the Elixir of Life. What does it feel like? What is it that you need to make this visualization a reality?

2. Imagine that your creative-sexual-etheric energy radiates outward from the sexual center and permeates your entire body, continuing to radiate in a bluish violet light (sometimes bluish gray, but it must be bright), interacting and penetrating everything it contacts.

3. Imagine your sense of self, your spiritual power, radiating out from your heart and permeating your entire body as a reddish golden light. Imagine that this light and energy continues outward, interacting and penetrating everything it contacts.

The Living Stone

Prepare yourself for meditation and then continue as follows:

1. Contemplate a brilliant sphere of light above your head for two or three minutes. Breathe in and feel the energy going directly toward your solar plexus, about three to four inches below the heart, and imagine a line of light in extension from above.

2. As you continue breathing, focus on your solar plexus and imagine that it is a brilliant sphere of red, reddish gold, or reddish purple light. Imagine and feel its magnetic field, and feel that it is a massive concentration of life energy.

3. Simply continue to breathe, either four-square or at your own rhythm; focus your whole being in your solar plexus with the feeling of perfect harmony, balance, and maximum life force concentrated within you.

4. As you progress, sense this focal point of energy growing strong and solid, and with it, its magnetic sphere penetrating in a spherical fashion your body and aura. Continue with this until you can easily sense your aura as having a firm surface about ten to twelve feet from you in all directions, filled with this powerful energy that radiates from the central "Stone" in your solar plexus.

Individual Mercury

1. Imagine a brilliant solar energy in the area of your heart. Feel its heat and warmth emanate outward. Feel the vast magnetic field of energy around it as you would feel the heat radiating from a lamp or an electric bulb. As you inhale, imagine the little sun growing brighter, and as you exhale, imagine its sphere of influence, the magnetic sphere radiating from and around it, expanding. Do this several times.

2. Move your attention to your head and imagine that there is a brilliant crescent moon in the center of it. Imagine it silvery white in color. Feel its cold, contracting nature, as if everything that comes near it is caught in its inward pull. Feel a cool magnetic field around it, which expands as you inhale and contracts more strongly as you exhale. Do this several times.

3. With your attention still focused on your head and the lunar crescent, imagine that the magnetic pull of the lunar energies brings the solar energies of the heart up to them as you exhale. Each time you inhale, the magnetic pull of the lunar energies increases, and as you exhale, the solar energies expand to meet or mingle with them.

4. Imagine now that these combined energies move down into your body, into the region of your solar plexus. As you inhale, the balanced lunar-solar energies grow stronger, and as you exhale, they are radiated throughout your physical body, even into the space around you.

5. Note any experiences you may have had when you have completed this meditation. Write them down in your notebook.

Meditation on Sulphur, Salt, and Mercury

Using the information contained in this chapter, develop your own meditations for the three essentials.

ten

ALCHEMICAL SYMBOLISM AND THE TAROT

Alchemy has been linked to Qabala since time immemorial. In addition to Hermetic references, several Jewish alchemical texts exist, further strengthening the connection. The most famous of these is a treatise on mineral alchemy, the *Aesch Mezareph*, or "Purifying Fire." However, for many, the

CHAPTER OVERVIEW
- *The Tarot as Hermetic Synthesis*
- *Alchemical Interpretation of the Major Arcana*
- *Symbolism, Dreams, and Inner Awakening*

link between Qabala and alchemy solidified in the fourteenth century, when Nicholas Flamel went to Spain in search of a Qabalistic rabbi to help him decode the strange engravings in the alchemical text that had dominated every waking hour of his and Perenelle's life for twenty-two years—the hieroglyphs in the Book of Abraham the Jew. (See Appendix C for more about Flamel.) Later, this information would be transferred to the Paths of the Tree of Life, thereby offering us insight into deciphering alchemical practices and general information about the principal alchemical paths known as the "Wet Way" and the "Dry Way."

However, it is only recently that tarot cards have been assimilated into Qabala, and as such, while offering us some alchemical information, the information is limited. For students with an affinity for the tarot, the images found in alchemical plates and texts will be a gold mine of symbolic opportunity. To help prepare you for working with these images in an alchemical fashion (rather than strictly Wiccan, Qabalistic, or as a fortune-telling device), we will briefly examine the tarot cards and interpret them according to the principles of physical and transcendental alchemy. In working with images that most students are already familiar with, we hope that their consciousness will be "seeded" with the process that is used in alchemical plates and engravings.

The Fool—This card represents the aspiring alchemist early in his or her journey, filled with visions of what is possible and completely ignorant of the reality of the inner and outer work that awaits.

The Magus—This card is the accomplished alchemist, creator of the Philosopher's Stone, master of the elements. It is what we aspire to become.

The Priestess—This card reveals the secrets of Nature to us. Through a study and application of the divine laws manifesting in our perceptions of the visible and invisible worlds, the veil of ignorance is pulled back, and Nature stands revealed in the Empress. The Priestess is linked to the Prima Materia, or First Matter of the Wise, and needs to be studied in this light. The Prima Materia is everywhere and can be had cheaply if we just know where to look and how to harness it. The lunar forces influencing our world are a microcosmic reflection of the greater principles demonstrated by this trump.

The Empress—The Empress is the Queen of Nature in her full glory. This represents the invisible energies operating in the material body and life of the alchemist. As generator of forms and substance, she is the Celestial Waters as well, or the Queen of Heaven hidden in the Priestess.

The Emperor—The Emperor is Aries, action, the first phase of the work. He is often associated with sulphur, the self-realizing power within everything. This is the essential vital energy needed to initiate, sustain, and complete the Great Work.

The Pope—Often called the Hierophant, or Teacher of the Mysteries, the Pope is a form of Thoth. He is also the great animating force in life, as is mercury to the plant, mineral, or animal realms. The self-realizing powers of self are drawn to it, as sulphur is to mercury, drawing the latent energies of sulphur (or consciousness) into fruition and expression through the power of motion and activity.

The Lovers—This card represents the two great paths of alchemy: the Wet Way and the Dry Way. The angel is the Inner Alchemist, the Holy Guardian Angel, who through intuition and dreams helps aspiring alchemists make their choices and find their way. One way is slow and sure; the other is fast and dangerous.

The Chariot—The Chariot represents the oven of the alchemist and its need to be constantly watched, directed, and controlled through skillful operations of the head, heart, and hands.

Justice—Every action has an equal and opposite reaction. The possible outcomes of every act must be understood to avoid error, accident, and disaster. The habits of mind, emotions, and action (karma) developed along the way are the sources of our balanced approach and keep us from being sidetracked.

The Hermit—The son of Hermes is an adept who is in, but not of, the world. He is seen but hidden from the eyes of the profane, or those who would seek to abuse the powers of Nature. The Hermit shuts himself off from the world, led by his inner light, relying on the staff of experience to create new and more perfect forms so that what is seeking expression in material life may be an improvement over what it replaces.

The Wheel of Fortune—The cycles of life are the source of misery and happiness in life. Through understanding and using them, the alchemist is able to stand outside the domain of fate and be master of life. Freedom from the Wheel is achieved by following the most propitious time for every act; in doing so, astrology is the friend and aid of the alchemist.

Strength—The most sublime of all cards, this synthesizes alchemy, astrology, and Qabala through the tarot. The woman, Sophia (Wisdom), directs the energies of instincts (the Lion), and in doing so commands the most difficult, powerful, and dangerous aspects of the work—the blind forces of matter and the subconscious. By using what energy we have available to us wisely, we gain more, and what once could destroy us now willingly serves and assists us in our undertakings.

The Hanged Man—This is the sign of sulphur, or self-realizing energies brought to fruition. In this, however, the world as it was known is turned upside down. The bonds of material life must be loosened—and in some instances lost—so that the energies may flow from the feet to the head, and the sublime work realized.

Death—Constant change is constant renewal, and death is the loosening of energies of matter for release into spirit and eventual rebirth. The dead matter gives up its spirit, just as the corpse gives up the consciousness of friend, stranger, and foe alike. If the spirit, however, has no new form to enter into, or the old one is not resurrected, then its energies are lost and the work is a failure and must be restarted. This card should be studied in relation to the Hanged Man and the Last Judgement.

Temperance—Constant flux and reflux of the active and passive forces is how the universe expresses itself in and through us. We must understand the cycles within ourselves and balance them if we are to become the Magus. This constant flux allows for spiritual and physical renewal and regeneration. The fluids and their vases are the lunar and solar energies that are manipulated through the two alchemical paths: the Dry Way, or "the foot on land," and the Wet Way, or "the foot in the water." Both belong to the adept once the other has been mastered, as the Philosopher's Stone belongs to both paths, and is one.

The Devil—"Solve et coagula" is a term you will hear often in alchemical work, and as was pointed out in chapter 2, it is the key to all occult work. Students of tarot see these words emblazoned on the arms of the Devil in the Oswald Wirth deck and other tarot decks derived from Qabala and alchemy. It is good to write this down on a card and place it where you can easily see it when you are doing your alchemical work. Just as the muscles of the human body grow stronger through the process of breaking down and building up, so do the powers of alchemical products grow more potent though an identical cycle of activity. This process is so fundamental to alchemy, and the plant experiments outlined here in particular, that a considerable amount of time should be spent meditating on this phrase. A copy of the fifteenth trump of the tarot can be used to assist in meditation, insofar as the typical descriptions given are ignored, and students seek to use it as a means of strictly alchemical insight into the hidden workings of Nature's invisible forces. Nothing is wasted, or evil in the true sense, and matter is put to the use of spirit.

The Tower—This card is the first disaster: the wrong intention for undertaking the work, inappropriate attention to details, haste, pride, and materialism corrupting the work.

The Star—This represents the influences of the astral energies though the planetary hours, the influences of the zodiac on alchemical work, the power of seasons, and the ever-present reality of the magnetic powers of Nature, or natural magic.

The Moon—This is the symbol of the White Stone and the Wet Way.

The Sun—This is the symbol of the Red Stone and the Dry Way.

Judgement—This represents discretion, reasoning, and the power of traditions brought forward into the modern world.

The World/Universe—This is the accomplishment of the Great Work, the Stone made and multiplied. The ideals of Chesed are manifest on earth, and the Hermit's journey is done.

The Fool—Whoso begins the journey and completes it. The seeker who began in ignorance has acquired wisdom. This is the Wise Man and the Fool in one. The alchemist at the beginning of the journey of the Path of Return completes it full of wisdom and grace. He is the Alpha and the Omega.

SYMBOLISM: THE LANGUAGE OF THE BIRDS

Symbols are the gateway to the psychic realms. The currency we pay to enter these realms is consistency. Symbols are often called the "language of the soul," and like any language of earth, symbols reflect a specific culture, history, and collective experience of the path they communicate. If you wish to be fluent in the use of symbols, you must treat them as you would any language or specialized area of study, and that means a consistent use of their meanings, colors, shapes, and forms.

The great strength of oriental iconography lies in its mathematical proportions and its use of color. Through a regular and repeated use of specific shapes, sizes, and colors, artists of different traditions pass on from generation to generation a symbolic language that connects them across the centuries. The same is true in any esoteric system, and no less so in alchemy.

In alchemy, this language became known as the "language of the birds" or the "green language." The symbolism is clear when we remember that the bird, or more specifically the dove, is the symbol of the Holy Spirit, the messenger of God, our intuition, and that green is the color of rebirth and vitality, one of the colors of the alchemist. The language's artistic high point was during the construction of the great Gothic cathedrals across Europe. It is not surprising that many of these cathedrals were built upon pre-Christian (specifically Druidic) sites, as well as what dowsers call ley lines, or magnetically sensitive areas of the earth. In *Points of Cosmic Energy*, Blanche Merz details these various connecting points between the invisible and visible on the earth's surface and demonstrates how current research has been able to identify the unique energetic qualities of them and their surrounding water supplies. In *Cathedral of the Black Madonna*, Jean Markale, a specialist in Celtic studies and author of over forty books, details the relationship between the early Druid priesthood of ancient France and the many architectural and spiritual mysteries surrounding Chartres, one of the greatest cathedrals of the High Middle Ages. However, it is the enigmatic alchemical author Fulcanelli that unites all of this information in a meaningful and practical manner for the aspiring alchemist.

Nothing is absolutely known about Fulcanelli. He is said to have been, or is, a French alchemist who wrote two books published in the early twentieth century: *The Mystery of the Cathedrals* and *The Dwellings of the Philosophers*. Both books discuss alchemical symbolism as it appears in architectural representations across France. Much speculation has grown up around Fulcanelli, including suggesting that he had completed the Great Work and lived in an alchemical retreat in Spain. Other suggestions are less dramatic, such as saying that Fulcanelli is the nom de plume for an author or group of authors seeking to preserve alchemical knowledge. Even his name—Fulcanelli—can be seen as a verbal symbol or play on words, combining "Vulcan," the ancient god of the forge and fire, and "El," a Hebrew word for God, thereby giving us the meaning "the forge of God." Regardless, the tradition of authors of alchemical works desiring anonymity is well established, and Fulcanelli follows in this tradition. Of his two books, *The Mystery of the Cathedrals* is the most impressive and useful to the beginning student of alchemical symbolism.[1]

Alchemical symbolism and dreams often use a play on words, in which "sounds like" is the meaning rather than "looks like." For example, in English, the third letter of the alphabet, a large body of

---

1 Much of this symbolism can be found in cathedrals in the United States, as they were copied from the European originals. It is suggested that entire cities have been built on esoteric symbolism, including Washington, D.C.

salt water, and the act of vision all sound alike: C, *sea*, and *see*. According to Fulcanelli, this ability to play with words creates a "phonetic cabala" or symbolic language that could be found in art, song, poetry, dreams, and mystical experiences.

This kind of transposition of sounds, meaning, and images is important when we deal with psychic phenomena, as the astral world is synthetic. Images and sounds are our chief forms of obtaining information in the material world. In the psychic, additional methods come into play that can be chaotic and confusing by mundane standards.

This is why it is impossible to interpret dreams if they are taken literally. The very nature of a dream is to be nonliteral. Other forms of psychic communication are more direct; however, time, patience, and experience are needed to be able to recognize and use them reliably.

LUCID DREAMING: GATEWAY TO THE ASTRAL

The only way to become an adept of any tradition is to become completely fluent in the symbolism of that tradition. The only way to become fluent in the symbolism of a tradition is to work with it. Just as we must practice our drills and conversation skills when learning a foreign language, the same applies to symbols.

Meditation and rituals are working aspects of symbols. Surrounding ourselves with esoteric art, making drawings, or copying and illuminating images in our notebooks is the process of imbibing, or immersing ourselves in a symbolic environment. Dreams and visions are the act of conversation and dialogue. It is here that we must learn to observe, listen, and remember so that we can interpret our dreams in a manner practical to our spiritual practice.

When interpreting dreams, four things are important:

1. Consistent symbolism.

2. Writing the dreams down.

3. Regular practice.

4. Using planetary hours to aid interpretation.

Consistent Symbolism

Consistent symbolism means giving the same meaning to a symbol, color, or sound and keeping it within its tradition, not seeking meaning elsewhere. This is difficult for many who seek to be eclectic and multicultural in their path. While it is fine to be broad-minded and tolerant on the intellectual level, at some point you have to make a decision about what you are going to do and how you are going to do it. This applies to the material domain as much as the psychic and the spiritual. If you choose to speak to someone using French vocabulary and Chinese grammar, with German conjugation thrown in, don't be surprised when they don't understand you. The same applies to our subconscious when it acts as the conduit between our mundane consciousness and our superconsciousness. The subconscious is synthetic. It does not rationalize. The more you fill it with, the more it will attempt to harmonize and make sense of the various disparate parts. If this is done as part of a specific system, then progress is made. If it is done haphazardly, then confusion results. Our ability to understand our dreams and the symbols they contain is a direct reflection of our personal integration. Consistency may be difficult—and boring at times—but it is the key to progress in this area.

Keep a notebook in which you write down symbols and their meanings. Use it as your personal dream dictionary. By doing this, you train your subconscious to use specific symbols in a specific manner so that they are meaningful to you.

To start the process, you can use some symbolic seed material. This includes:

A Dictionary of Symbolism, by J. E. Cirlot

The Mystery of the Cathedrals, by Fulcanelli, translated by Mary Sworder (The American edition is also known under the title *Fulcanelli: Master Alchemist.*)

The Alchemical Mandala, by Adam McLean

Godwin's Cabalistic Encyclopedia, by David Godwin

The Tarot of the Magicians, by Oswald Wirth

The Golden Game: Alchemical Engravings of the Seventeenth Century,
   by Stanislas Klossowski de Rola

Writing Them Down

If it is important enough to dream, it is important enough to write
down. The act of writing down a dream, even a fragment, is a message to the subconscious that this information is important and to
keep it coming. By writing down our dreams, we "fix" the "volatile"
message that our Inner Mercury, or Messenger of the Gods, is bringing us.

Regular Practice

Dreams can be stimulated through a variety of practices that fall under the broad heading of dream yoga, or "Union through Dreams."
This union is with none other than our own Inner Self. Through
repeated practice, we can come to communicate directly with this
aspect of our self, transcending even dreams and symbols in direct
language and experience.

   Dream practices can be very simple and direct to be effective. The
following method will assist in jump-starting your dreaming memory
and even dream lucidity. Astral projection may also occur as a result
of this practice. The nice thing about dream practices is that we must
sleep, so spending a few minutes as we lie in bed directing our consciousness to assist us in our work is about as passive a practice as
there is on the path to enlightenment.

Dream Practice

1. As you lie in bed, focus your attention on your throat, behind
   the Adam's apple, where the thyroid gland is. Imagine a sphere
   of brilliant orange or red-orange light. This can be small, but
   it radiates a large sphere of influence in its aura. This sphere
   can extend from just above your sternum to below the bridge

of your nose if you want to imagine it. Otherwise, simply stay with the brilliant sphere of light.

2. Verbally, silently, or in a whisper, recite the following affirmation: "Tonight I will dream, and I will remember my dreams." This affirmation can be made more specific with experience to include the following: "Tonight I will dream, and I will become aware that I am dreaming." Or it can be used to continue with a dream that left off from a previous night: "Tonight I will dream, and my dream will continue from this point [imagine the end of the dream you wish to use as a pickup point]." You may repeat this three or seven times with confidence that you will dream.

3. Write down any dream experiences you have during the night.

The process can be more complex and developed as dream practices begin to involve lucid dreaming, astral projection, and heightened states of consciousness. However, they all rely on this basic technique as their foundation.[2]

Planetary Hours

One of the most confusing aspects of dream interpretation occurs when dreams appear to be fragments of other dreams and we seek to link them together but don't know how. We may have a dream on Monday, another on Tuesday, and a third on Friday. We write them down and line them up like chapters in a book, but instead of making any sense, it looks like we pulled three chapters at random from a book on history, a romance novel, and a physics textbook. We convince ourselves that it is hopeless and that we will never understand our dreams, and we go back to forgetting them. However, just as planetary energies affect our alchemical and meditative work, they also affect our dream work. If we took those three "chapters"

---

2 For more information, see: "A Qabalistic Guide to Lucid Dreaming," by Mark Stavish, at www.hermeticinstitute.org (look for the link to online articles under Hermetic Resources).

and, instead of lining them up, put them back in the proper "books" in which they belong, we could begin to make sense of their messages. For this reason, when you write down your dreams, keep the planetary day and night in mind. Saturday at sunrise until Sunday at sunrise is ruled by Saturn. Therefore, all dreams on a Saturday night or early Sunday morning, before sunrise, are influenced by Saturn. Dreams in the morning—at or after sunrise—will be influenced by the new planetary energies. In summertime, in areas where daylight-savings time is used, the sun may rise at 5:00 a.m. If you sleep until 7:00 a.m. and know that your dream occurred just before waking, it is important to analyze it in relation to the new energies. However, many people dream sometime between 3:00 a.m. and 5:00 a.m., thereby eliminating this problem.

Once you record a dream, make sure that you connect your dreams according to the planetary days. A dream on Saturday night should be followed by any dream that may occur on each succeeding Saturday. The same applies for each of the remaining days of the week.

These dreams should be read as chapters, then, in your personal "planetary dream book." They should also be reviewed prior to sleep to stimulate your subconscious with the leaving-off point of the last dream as the starting point of the next dream in the series.

As an example of an alchemical dream interpretation, the following dream was experienced by a practitioner of alchemy while performing a specific operation. The dream occurred on a Sunday night in April, during a waxing Moon, with Mercury retrograde. The weather was very damp and chilly.

Dream

"I am in the basement of my house, distilling a product. It is not clear if it is red wine or another tincture, but the color is dark and rich. The basement is different from normal, in that it is all dirt; brown predominates, and the space is completely empty except for a small distillation setup before me and the stairs behind me. They are not directly behind me, but instead are at an angle and go up and to my (back-facing) left. To my (front-facing) left is a bare light bulb on a cord.

"I reach for the light bulb with some hesitation, as something doesn't feel right. I realize that some force or energy is present with me. I turn and run up the stairs toward the exit. Just as the door is about to close, I force it open, and in doing so experience a sphere of energy around me of tremendous power. I stop and feel proud of my achievement—an almost 'showed you' attitude—then exit."

Interpretation

Interpreting a dream is easy once we identify the key symbols and link them together like words in a sentence or ideas in a story. Here are the key symbols as identified by the dreamer in this dream.

Basement of my house—*House* is "Beth" in Hebrew, and also the Moon. The basement is the supporting structure, or foundation (Yesod). This is the dreamer's subconscious.

Distilling a product whose color is dark and rich—A work of purification has reached a critical or possibly end stage.

All dirt; brown predominates—The place of "work" is the material world. This dream conveys a very concrete lesson.

Empty except for a small distillation setup before me—The lesson is simple and the teaching direct. There is nothing to distract the dreamer's attention.

Stairs are behind me at an angle and go up and to my (back-facing) left—The dreamer is isolated. Leaving is not simple. Left is the direction of mercy, or divine grace. It could also be a symbolic direction in the language of the birds, that is, "left" as in past tense of "to leave."

To my (front-facing) left is a bare light bulb on a cord—Light, similar to the tarot card of the Hermit when the dreamer reaches for it. The outer light is touched and left behind, and the inner light must be relied upon when the force of the dream is awakened.

Experience a sphere of energy around me of tremendous power—The energy aroused is absorbed, or assimilated in some fashion, but is more indirect than direct.

I stop and feel proud of my achievement—From fear to pride in a split second! Human folly.

Dream Summary

The dreamer is purifying a product that relates to the Inner Self, connection to the root of his being. Progress requires greater isolation and inward presence, but also a connection to the concrete and material. The work awakens great energy and potential, but also with it great fear of the very thing that is sought. The mind must cease to be afraid of the energies that give it life. Once aroused, these energies cannot be escaped but must be absorbed and assimilated. The absurdity of the dreamer's ego is that it moves from fear of its own creation to pride over vanquishing it inside of an instant. This hints at the dangers of human activities in the esoteric realms. The greatest threat to all spiritual work is pride. The test must be repeated. Much of the symbolism hints at the tarot card for the Hermit: Yod, Virgo, Mercury, Earth, ascent, light before and above or at the level of the head, Mercury retrograde.

ALCHEMICAL PATHWORKING

The use of guided visualizations in Qabala is referred to as pathworking and consists of a series of interrelated symbols given in connection with a particular story. Each story is nearly identical in context, in that it has a beginning, an obstacle, the resolution of the obstacle, a reward for overcoming the obstacle, and completion or return. The content changes from pathworking to pathworking to reflect the various experiences one will encounter along the spiritual path. Alchemy has similar stories, both verbal and visual, in which the process of transmutation is detailed in the form of one or more interlocking stories. Short verses of poetry or prose may accompany each symbolic scene, as in Salomon Trismosin's *Splendor Solis*, or, like in the *Mutus Liber*, there may be nothing except images. Regardless, the ability to imaginatively enter into a scene, bring it to life, and extract information psychically from it is critical to the alchemical process. The following exercise will assist in developing a sense of the similarity between alchemical images and Qabalistic pathworking, particularly those systems utilizing the images from the tarot trumps. It is important that the images be visualized in both the third person and first person. Look at the images and what they are doing, and then become the images and observe what you as the image or character are doing.

The following exercise is taken from the images found in the *Splendor Solis*, an alchemical manuscript dating to at least the mid-sixteenth century. The *Splendor Solis* is one of the most famous alchemical manuscripts because of its twenty-two beautiful color plates, which are fully reproduced in *Art and Symbols of the Occult: Images of Power and Wisdom*, by James Wasserman. The *Splendor Solis* was a document much studied by some of the key figures in the early Hermetic Order of the Golden Dawn. Reverend W. A. Ayton's pupil, Julius Kohn, was responsible for its first modern publication and translation in 1920, and S. L. MacGregor Mathers valued it highly enough to work on a translation reportedly published in 1907. Unfortunately, copies of Mathers's limited edition have not surfaced. The most recent edition of the *Splendor Solis* was translated by Joscelyn Godwin with commentary by Adam McLean and published by Phanes Press; however, its plates are in black and white. Copies of the color images can also be found on McLean's alchemy website.

Exercise

1. Prepare yourself for meditation.
2. Imagine a glass egg or retort before you. Carefully build the image in detail.

3. Imagine yourself passing through the glass and entering the egg. There, in the center of the egg, you hover above the dark waters filling the lower third of the vessel.

4. Imagine that you are a small, naked child, like the cherubim often portrayed in Renaissance art. You hold a pair of bellows and are pumping them. Before you is a yellow dragon, and your bellows are pointed at its chest. As you pump the bellows, the dragon goes from yellow to a bright red.

5. The red dragon now transforms into three birds: one red, one white, and one black. They are intertwined and are pecking at each other.

6. The heat increases, and the three birds become one body and three heads, colored white. Each head bears a golden crown.

7. Again the heat increases, and the bird is transformed into a yellow dragon with three heads: one white, one black, and one red.

8. The heat increases, transforming the dragon into a peacock with its tail in full bloom.

9. The peacock transforms into a queen in a white dress, breasts bare, a crown upon her head and facing to her right. She holds a golden wand in her left hand and an orb in her right hand. The orb is before her belly, and she is surrounded by an aura of yellow edged with an equal amount of light blue. She stands upon a crescent moon, horns upturned (Tail of the Dragon).

10. For a final time, the heat increases, and the queen is transformed into a king in a red cape and robes. He wears a golden crown and holds an orb topped with a small equal-armed cross (the symbol of terrestrial victory, also antimony) in his left hand and a golden wand in his right. He stands upon an inverted crescent moon, horns turned down (Head of the Dragon), and he is surrounded by a brilliant golden aura.

11. After a period of time, exit the egg.

12. Write down your experiences, the date and time of the meditation, and the lunar cycle.

KEY POINTS

- Symbols are the language of the subconscious.

- Traditional astrological and Qabalistic tarot symbols can act as a bridge into alchemy.

- The major arcana of the tarot cards can be read in relation to alchemy.

- Regular meditation on symbols improves dream life and increases intuition.

- The symbolic languages of alchemy and dreams are identical, and this language is referred to as the "language of the birds" and the "green language" in traditional sources.

- Dream practices can increase dream regularity, memory, and lucidity and can ultimately lead to astral projection.

- It is important to create your own dictionary of symbols for your dream interpretation.

- The four keys to success in interpreting dreams are consistency in symbolic interpretation, regular dream practices, writing down dreams, and using planetary correspondences to link dreams from week to week rather than in a linear progression across one week.

GENERAL ASSIGNMENTS FOR CHAPTER TEN

1. Obtain a deck of tarot cards. The Oswald Wirth deck is preferred; however, the Tarot of Marseille or the Rider-Waite deck will also do. Examine the cards in light of the brief alchemical notation given them in this chapter. Use only traditional decks for this exercise. Write, draw, or photocopy and paste these cards and the information in your notebook.

2. Obtain one or more of the books or courses mentioned in this chapter and begin the construction of your personal dictionary of symbols.

3. Pick a recent dream that you have experienced and, using the example in this chapter, write it down, using bullet points to note the key ideas. Interpret the events in as few words as possible and then synthesize the ideas into one or two sentences (or words if possible). Distill the meaning of dreams; obtain their essence.

4. Begin recording your dreams in the manner outlined in this chapter.

MEDITATION PRACTICES FOR CHAPTER TEN

1. Begin a nightly dream practice as outlined in this chapter.

2. Meditate with the various tarot cards and the alchemical descriptions given in this chapter, and notice your reaction to the ideas presented.

Conclusion

The reader who has completed this book by now realizes that alchemy is a lifelong process. Even if the Philosopher's Stone is had in twenty-two years, as with Flamel, it is still a lifetime of investment that has gone into obtaining such Illumination. Given the potential complexity of alchemical work, the procedures described here are sufficient to keep the aspiring alchemist busy for a year or more, simply working to feel comfortable with the process. It can then take several additional years to become fully competent with these procedures in practice. However, do not be discouraged by these statements. Remember, a little bit of work done regularly goes much further than a lot of work performed in a short period of time. Alchemy cannot be rushed. This simple truth is easily demonstrated in the creation of spagyric medicines, as well as in their use. When taken regularly over a period of time, they have an accumulative effect. While the individual doses may wear off after a week or so, each time a medicine is ingested, the organs of spiritual perception are flexed a little more and, like physical muscles, grow stronger. Like any study worth undertaking, patience, confidence, faith, and grace are the tools needed. How can it be any less when we are talking of the Great Work? Yet in the end, it is ourselves we transmute. The plants and minerals are just our helpers along the way.

The journey is also one that, while we may begin it with the most selfish of reasons and intentions—health, wealth, or power—becomes a selfless one in the end. The rough edges of our personality are slowly worn down, the very force that drives us toward success exhausts itself in the process, and we find ourselves at the doorstep of adepthood caring more about others than our own final victory.

This kind of journey was hinted at by Paracelsus when, in chapter 8 of his work *De Minerabilis*, he predicted the return of Elias Artista, or Elias the Artist. Paracelsus referred to this futuristic Hermetic adept in messianic terms: "A symbol of the ripeness of the age! He is the great day to come when all secrets shall be brought to light, and things now rooting in the dark earth shall be brought to light, and things now rooting in the dark earth shall come forth to full growth and flower and bear a treasure, which is for the healing of nations . . . a symbolic representation, the collective breath of generous vindications. Spirit of Liberty, of science and love which must regenerate the world!"[3]

Yet regardless, no one can do the work for us. Like Paracelsus, Flamel, and others, Elias the Artist can only be a teacher of the method. It is up to each of us to develop it and make it our own. In doing the work, we open ourselves up to the light within ourselves, and we are also able to recognize the light in others. It is this recognition that brings us to the domain of the adepts, not as a beggar but as a mature and capable student—or an equal.

May all who read this book and undertake the Great Work come to a "Good End."

Finis

---

3 Robert A. Nelson, *Prophecy: A History of the Future* (Rex Research, 2000), chap. 3, http://www.rexresearch.com/prophist/phf3eu~1.htm (accessed July 7, 2006).

appendix A

PLANETARY HOURS

Planetary hours are a critical part of natural magic and alchemy. While there are systems of magic that do not take them into account, the majority of systems of occultism currently practiced make some reference to them. There are in fact two systems for calculating planetary hours for each day. One system is fixed, with each day beginning at 6:00 a.m. and ending twenty-four hours later, but this system is rarely used. In the more common system, each day begins at sunrise and continues until sunrise of the following morning. This means that the length of each planetary hour in each day will change with the seasons and needs to be calculated every few days to take into accordance the change in the amount of sunlight each day possesses.

Despite appearances, calculating planetary hours is simple, and an entire week can be calculated fairly quickly using one set of numbers. You may want to advance it one minute for each additional day. However, operations rarely start exactly on the time calculated for an hour. It is best to be prepared and wait a few minutes for the inner response that the time has begun. This can be as much as ten minutes after the calculated time. Sunrise and sunset times are often listed in local newspapers.

1. Starting with Saturday, find the actual time of sunrise.

2. Find the actual time of sunset.

3. Find the time for sunrise on Sunday.

These three times establish the length of a planetary hour.

1. Take the period from sunrise to sunset and calculate the number of minutes involved.

2. Divide this number by 12. This will give you the length in actual minutes of each planetary hour for the daytime period.

3. Subtract the daytime number of minutes from 1,440 (the number of minutes in a twenty-four-hour period) to derive the length of the evening period.

4. Divide this number by 12. This will give you the length in actual minutes of the planetary hours for the night.

5. Based on the actual time of sunrise, graph your hours and the times they occur. Repeat this for the nighttime hours.

Example

If sunrise on Saturday is at 5:28 a.m. and sunset is at 6:30 p.m., we have 772 minutes of sunlight. This gives us 12 hours of slightly under 65 minutes each. So, our first hour begins at 5:28 a.m. and ends at 6:33 a.m. Our second hour begins at 6:33 a.m. and ends at 7:38 a.m., and so on until all 12 planetary hours of the day are calculated. With sunset at 6:30 p.m. and using the same sunrise for Sunday as on Saturday, we have 668 minutes of nighttime. We divide 668 by 12 for the hours of the night and get slightly over 55 minutes in a planetary hour, and this we round up to 56 minutes. Our first hour of the night begins at 6:30 p.m. and ends at 7:26 p.m.; our second hour begins at 7:26 p.m. and ends at 8:22 p.m.; and so on.

The order of the planets begins on Saturday and follows the Tree of Life, giving us Saturn, Jupiter, Mars, Sun, Venus, Mercury, Moon for the first seven hours and then simply repeating the cycle across every hour of every day of the week. This has the unique result of the first hour of each day corresponding to its rulership. As such, the first hour of each day will always be Saturn for Saturday, Sun for Sunday, Moon for Monday, Mars for Tuesday, Mercury for Wednesday, Jupiter for Thursday, and Venus for Friday. The first hour of every night will always be Mercury for Saturday, Jupiter for Sunday,

Venus for Monday, Saturn for Tuesday, Sun for Wednesday, Moon for Thursday, and Mars for Friday.

Study the charts that follow and practice calculating planetary hours until you can be sure that your calculations match the flow of the planets outlined.

Calculating Exact Planetary Hours

The reason there is a delay between the calculated beginning of the planetary hour and the actual beginning of an operation is to allow for the natural rotation of the earth and its reception of planetary energies to "catch up" with the artificial timelines established. If you want to calculate the actual beginning of a planetary hour in coordination with local time, you need to know the longitude of the location you are calculating for. Four minutes is deducted from Greenwich Mean Time for each degree the location is west of Greenwich, and four minutes added for each minute east of Greenwich. This will allow you to calculate an exact beginning and end to planetary hours.

Table One

The table on the next page shows the planetary hours for one day. The day is a Friday, because the first hour of the day is Venus. The first hour lasts from 6:12 a.m. until 7:23 a.m. and is 71 minutes long; the hour that follows, a Mercury hour, starts at 7:23 and continues until 8:33 a.m.; and so forth. If we examine the exact point at which the daylight hours have reached their halfway point, we find true Mid Day or Noon, which for this day falls on a solar hour. True Mid Night falls at the halfway point of the nighttime hours, which are shorter, and comes during a Jupiter hour. For the majority of work done in spagyrics, alchemy, talismans, and various forms of planetary magic, this simple breakdown of the planetary hours across the day is all that is needed. However, those seeking a more advanced use of the hours can use an extended breakout.

Simple Version

Ve	~~6:12~~
Me	7:23
Lu	8:33
Sa	9:44
Ju	10:54
Ma	12:04
So	13:15
Ve	14:25
Me	15:36
Lu	16:46
Sa	17:57
Ju	19:07
Ma	20:17
So	21:07
Ve	21:57
Me	22:46
Lu	23:36
Sa	0:26
Ju	1:15
Ma	2:05
So	2:55
Ve	3:44
Me	4:34
Lu	5:24
Sa	6:13

Detailed Version

Each day and hour is ruled by the passing of the elements as well as the planets. The daylight hours are ruled by the active energies of fire and air, while the nighttime energies are ruled by the passive energies of water and earth. Each element rules six hours of planetary time. In addition, each hour can be further broken down into discrete segments of elemental influences and synthesized by the energies of Spirit. These elements are symbolized in the following chart by the Hebrew letters Heh (earth), Vau (water), Heh (air), Yod (fire), and Shin (Spirit), which are read from left to right to match the progression of the hour from start to finish.

From this information, is it possible to create a tincture, in this case a Venus tincture, that is biased toward an element by changing the period of the day or night it is started under, as well as adding in some additional planetary influences if the hour is moved from a Venus hour to one supportive of the function of the tincture. For example, a tincture oriented toward magic, but with the intention of being very psychic in nature, could be started during the water phase of the day and under a lunar influence. This hour starts at 23:36, or 11:36 p.m. If additional secondary effects are desired, such as material (earth), emotional (water), intellectual (air), spiritual (fire), or harmonizing (Spirit), the appropriate time within the hour to begin the operation can be discovered as well. Using these smaller units of time across the hour can be tricky; however, it is worthwhile to use them several times to gain the experience. In general, using the dominant elemental influence of the phase in which one works during the daytime or nighttime hours is sufficient modification to the work at hand.

		ה	ו	ה	י	ש
△		E	W	A	F	Q
	Ve	~~6:12~~	~~6:26~~	~~6:40~~	~~6:55~~	~~7:09~~
	Me	7:23	7:37	7:51	8:05	8:19
	Lu	8:33	8:47	9:01	9:15	9:29
	Sa	9:44	9:58	10:12	10:26	10:40
	Ju	10:54	11:08	11:22	11:36	11:50
	Ma	12:04	12:19	12:33	12:47	13:01
△	So	13:15	13:29	13:43	13:57	14:11
	Ve	14:25	14:39	14:53	15:08	15:22
	Me	15:36	15:50	16:04	16:18	16:32
	Lu	16:46	17:00	17:14	17:28	17:43
	Sa	17:57	18:11	18:25	18:39	18:53
	Ju	19:07	19:21	19:35	19:49	20:03
	Ma	20:17	20:27	20:37	20:47	20:57
	So	21:07	21:17	21:27	21:37	21:47
▽	Ve	21:57	22:07	22:17	22:27	22:36
	Me	22:46	22:56	23:06	23:16	23:26
	Lu	23:36	23:46	23:56	0:06	0:16
	Sa	0:26	0:36	0:46	0:55	1:05
	Ju	1:15	1:25	1:35	1:45	1:55
	Ma	2:05	2:15	2:25	2:35	2:45
	So	2:55	3:05	3:14	3:24	3:34
▽	Ve	3:44	3:54	4:04	4:14	4:24
	Me	4:34	4:44	4:54	5:04	5:14
	Lu	5:24	5:33	5:43	5:53	6:03
	Sa	6:13	This is the first hour of the next morning			

Mid Day (aligned with So row, 13:15–14:11)

Mid Night (aligned with Ju row, 1:15–1:55)

Table Two

Planetary Hours of the Day

Hour	Sunday	Monday	Tuesday	Wednesday	Thursday	Friday	Saturday
1	Sun	Moon	Mars	Mercury	Jupiter	Venus	Saturn
2	Venus	Saturn	Sun	Moon	Mars	Mercury	Jupiter
3	Mercury	Jupiter	Venus	Saturn	Sun	Moon	Mars
4	Moon	Mars	Mercury	Jupiter	Venus	Saturn	Sun
5	Saturn	Sun	Moon	Mars	Mercury	Jupiter	Venus
6	Jupiter	Venus	Saturn	Sun	Moon	Mars	Mercury
7	Mars	Mercury	Jupiter	Venus	Saturn	Sun	Moon
8	Sun	Moon	Mars	Mercury	Jupiter	Venus	Saturn
9	Venus	Saturn	Sun	Moon	Mars	Mercury	Jupiter
10	Mercury	Jupiter	Venus	Saturn	Sun	Moon	Mars
11	Moon	Mars	Mercury	Jupiter	Venus	Saturn	Sun
12	Saturn	Sun	Moon	Mars	Mercury	Jupiter	Venus

Planetary Hours of the Night

Hour	Sunday	Monday	Tuesday	Wednesday	Thursday	Friday	Saturday
1	Jupiter	Venus	Saturn	Sun	Moon	Mars	Mercury
2	Mars	Mercury	Jupiter	Venus	Saturn	Sun	Moon
3	Sun	Moon	Mars	Mercury	Jupiter	Venus	Saturn
4	Venus	Saturn	Sun	Moon	Mars	Mercury	Jupiter
5	Mercury	Jupiter	Venus	Saturn	Sun	Moon	Mars
6	Moon	Mars	Mercury	Jupiter	Venus	Saturn	Sun
7	Saturn	Sun	Moon	Mars	Mercury	Jupiter	Venus
8	Jupiter	Venus	Saturn	Sun	Moon	Mars	Mercury
9	Mars	Mercury	Jupiter	Venus	Saturn	Sun	Moon
10	Sun	Moon	Mars	Mercury	Jupiter	Venus	Saturn
11	Venus	Saturn	Sun	Moon	Mars	Mercury	Jupiter
12	Mercury	Jupiter	Venus	Saturn	Sun	Moon	Mars

THE LONGEVITY FORMULA OF COMTE DE ST. GERMAIN

The following formula has been circulating in modern Rosicrucian circles for decades and is attributed to the famous eighteenth-century alchemist—and purported Rosicrucian and Freemason—Comte de St. Germain. This recipe has been given to the author by several alchemists, each confirming the source and means of its transmission back to eighteenth-century Holland. A nearly identical recipe is cited on page 270 in *Comte de St. Germain: Last Scion of the House of Rakoczy*, by Jean Overton Fuller, the difference being a possible confusion between anise and fennel, as both herbs smell very similar. Fuller mentions preparing the tea in red wine by letting it soak for several hours and then straining it. It can also be placed on a very low heat. An easier method is to make a weak tea using distilled water and, again, strain the mixture prior to ingesting. The taste is soft and pleasant; honey can be added for flavor but is not needed. A careful examination of the recipe shows that the tea is designed to remove mucus, improve digestion, and stimulate regularity of the bowels.

Senna—2 grams

Elder flower—4 grams

Anise—1 gram

Manna—15 grams

(Manna is *Fraxinus ornus* and is often imported from Sicily.)

THE PATH OF NICHOLAS FLAMEL AND THE PHILOSOPHER'S STONE

Nicholas Flamel (also spelled Flammel) was born at Pontoise, France, in 1330. Little is known of his life prior to his undertaking the study of alchemy. However, as a result of his subsequent fame, the Bibliotheque Nationale in Paris contains copies of works made by him, as well as his own writings, in addition to his marriage certificate, deeds for gifts made while alive, and his last will and testament.

Flamel made his living as a scrivener, notary, and bookseller, with a stall that backed onto the columns of St. Jacques la Boucherie and measured little more than two and a half feet by two feet, or slightly larger than a telephone booth. He was also skilled in painting and poetry. As literacy was limited, even among the commercial and ruling classes, it was possible to make a modest living by reading and writing letters or documents for a fee or by teaching writing to those who were required to sign documents.

Flamel later purchased a house, possibly with the assistance of his wealthy wife, a widow several years his senior, and used the ground floor for business. Several employees were retained, and business was good.

It is known that he was born, like many, into poverty but was fortunate enough to have parents who instilled within him the virtues of honesty and ethics. He was able to acquire an education, and as such he moved to Paris, where he made his living. Like many in his occupation, he lived on the Street of the Notaries, near the Chapel of St. James of the Bouchery. Flamel's fortunes changed in 1357, when according to his own account he purchased a large, heavily gilded book for two florins. The book's cover was made of brass (or copper) and engraved with various symbols and letters. The pages were made of very thin leaves of bark, each being covered with beautifully drawn and colored symbols and text.

Every seventh page was free from any writing, holding only a picture. The first image was a serpent swallowing rods; the second, a serpent crucified on a cross; and the third, a vast desert with a bubbling fountain surrounded by serpents. The book appeared to have been written for the expert, at least in Qabala,[1] and assumed a knowledge of alchemy, and possibly even success in the art.

On the title page, the following was written in gold: *Abraham the Jew, Prince, Priest, Levite, Astrologer, and Philosopher, to the Nation of the Jews, by the Wrath of God dispersed among the Gentiles, sendeth Health.* The book was unlike anything being produced in Europe at that time, or previously, and suggests Middle Eastern origins.

According to the text, Abraham the Jew, its author, undertook the process of creating gold through transmutation to relieve the Jews of the burden imposed upon them by excessive taxation while in European lands—lands ruled by Christian monarchs who not only oppressed the Jews but also used such "taxes" collected to finance Christian churches and institutions. To help his fellow Jews deal with the burden placed upon them while in the Diaspora, the author gave the method of transmutation to his people.

---

1 Raphael Patai, *The Jewish Alchemists* (Princeton, NJ: Princeton University Press, 1994), 229. In the Book of Abraham the Jew, there are directions for the construction of a mirror to assist the alchemist in attaining insight into the work through communication with one or more angels. This is common in medieval and later Renaissance magical operations, and it continues to this day in the form of crystal gazing. The four names used in the preparation of the mirror are Jehovah, Elohim, Adonai, and Metatron, in the upper left, right, lower left, and right, respectively. One is to call out, "Come, O Angel Anael, in the name of the terrible Jehovah." There is also a conjuration of Raphael.

The word *Maranatha* was repeated many times on the pages, adding to the allure of the book. *Maranatha*, believed to be a curse or malediction equivalent to referring to the person as excrement, in its Aramaic original is actually a blessing. *Maranatha* is composed of two words, *maran* and *atha*, and means "The Lord has come!" or "Oh Lord come." This misuse of the word in the text suggests either a non-Jewish origin of Abraham the Jew's book or later Christian interpolation.[2] Despite this flaw, authentic Hebrew sentiments are stated elsewhere in the text.

However, what makes this book so special, so unique to Flamel, is that he was waiting for it to arrive. In his book *Lives of the Alchemystical Philosophers*, Arthur Edward Waite recounts a story regarding a vision Flamel had prior to acquiring the book that led to his success. An angel named Bath-Kol[3] appeared to Flamel, holding a book similar to the one he would later purchase, engraved with an iron pen, and said, "Flamel! Behold this book of which thou understandeth nothing; to many others but thyself it would remain forever unintelligible, but one day thou shalt discern in its pages that none but thyself shall see."[4] In Flamel's dream, he reached for the book, only to find that it and the angel disappeared in a radiant flash of light.

While dreams such as this appear throughout the Hermetic tradition and are familiar to students of Qabala, Rosicrucianism, and alchemy, in this case, we know the book Flamel would later find—and it exists to this day. For twenty-one years, Flamel studied the book, even painting its images on the walls of his home.

---

2 Ibid., 219.

3 Bath-Kol, if this is the proper spelling, is Hebrew for "Daughter of All." The gematria for it is 452 and reduces to 11, which has a numerological association with the ideas of concealment and gold. For Aleister Crowley, 11 represents the "special fire or light" of the Sacred Magic of Light, Life, and Love; hence "Odic Force," etc. If the spelling is instead the phonetically similar Bath-Qol, then it means "Daughter of the Voice" and is the voice of God from between the Cherubim of the Ark. It is the Shekinah, the Presence of God, and has the numerological value of 538, reducing to 16 and 7. See: David Godwin, *Godwin's Cabalistic Encyclopedia*, 3rd ed. (St. Paul, MN: Llewellyn Publications, 1994).

4 As mentioned in Manly P. Hall, *Orders of the Great Work* (Los Angeles: Philosophical Research Society, 1949), 53.

Flamel was no doubt familiar with alchemy, as books on it abound, and he possessed manuscripts on it himself, but the images in this book were a mystery to him. What he lacked was knowledge of Jewish mysticism.

Christian scholars were unable to help Flamel decipher the book's meaning, so he sought out a rabbi who could help him. Unfortunately for Flamel, the Jews had been driven out of France by brutal and systematic persecution. Massacres, imprisonment, expulsions, confiscation of property, and heavy fines were common. Since the chief rabbis were in Spain, it is there that Flamel went. He met a sage and was rewarded with success within three years after his return to Paris.

Many Jews had emigrated to Spain, settling in Granada and Malaga, where Moorish rulers were more tolerant than their Catholic neighbors to the north. In these areas, Jewish communities flourished, producing learned scholars, physicians, and Qabalists.

Traveling under the cloak of a pilgrim, with staff, shell, and hat, and carrying a few carefully copied pages of the book hidden on his person, Flamel headed toward Galacia. At the time of his journey, he would be nearly fifty years of age.

His welcome was not a warm one, as Jews made to leave their native France would hardly be inviting to a Christian poking around in their new homeland. Discouragement seemed to overtake Flamel. On his return journey through Leon, he stopped at an inn and had the good fortune to share the evening's table with a merchant, also French, who was from Boulogne. After a discussion of their reasons for traveling—the merchant on business, Flamel seeking a wise Jew— the merchant informed him of an associate of his who could help him, an old scholar and Qabalist known as Master Canches. The merchant offered to introduce Flamel to him.

Master Canches was impressed with the few pages Flamel had brought and decided despite his age to travel with him to Paris. Conveniently, he was also a convert to Catholicism. This may have been a genuine conversion or simply one of convenience, an insurance policy against further troubles. Canches's health faded over the course of the journey, and after seven days of vomiting and delirium, he died in Orleans. Flamel arranged for him to be buried in the Church of St. Croix, with accompanying masses. Flamel had learned enough from Master Canches so that upon his return home he was able to return to his work and studies with the confidence that he would be able to decipher the remaining pages.

After three more years of work, he and Perenelle were crowned with success: on Monday, January 17, 1382, at noon, according to Flamel, he succeeded in making a projection on mercury into silver. The following April 25, at 5:00 p.m., he converted mercury into gold. Only two additional accounts are known of the projection powder being used to make gold. Each time, the proceeds were used for charitable purposes. The lifestyle of Nicholas and Perenelle did not change after their alchemical success blessed them.

AFTER THE STONE IS MADE

Perenelle assisted in the experiments, and since they had no children, they donated their wealth, endowing churches and hospitals and restoring cemeteries, as was the custom of the day.

In Flamel's own words: "Before I wrote this commentary, which was toward the end of the year 1314, after the passing of my faithful companion, whom I shall lament all the days of my life, she and I had already founded and endowed fourteen hospitals, had built three Chapels and provided seven Churches with substantial gifts and revenues, as well as restoring their cemeteries."[5]

Louis Figuier, a historian, wrote: "Husband and wife lavished succor on the poor,[6] founded hospitals, built or repaired cemeteries, restored the front of St. Genevieve des Ardents and endowed the institution of the Quinze-Vingts, the blind inmates of which, in memory

---

5 Archibald Cockren, *Alchemy Rediscovered and Restored* (Whitefish, MT: Kessinger Publishing, n.d.), 38.

6 One of these "poorhouses" is now the oldest house in Paris, currently a restaurant.

of this fact, came every year to the church of St. Jacques la Boucherie to pray for their benefactor, a practice which continued until 1789."[7]

The couple's generosity aroused suspicion and attracted attention. A bookseller who had endowed so many social and religious institutions and undertaken public works to ease the suffering of the poor must have a secret indeed, and Charles VI ordered an investigation into the matter. Fortunately for Nicholas and Perenelle, the results of the investigation were favorable toward them.

LUCAS, AND THE SURVIVAL OF NICHOLAS AND PERENELLE

Under a commission from Louis XIV, Sieur Paul Lucas (1664–1737) traveled in search of antiquities, visiting Macedonia, Greece, Turkey, Asia Minor, and Africa. On his return, he, like all good travelers of the day, published a memoir of his journey, titled *Voyage de sieur Paul Lucas, Par ordre du Roi dans la Crece, etc.* (Amsterdam, 1712). The book was dedicated to his sponsor, Louis XIV. Given Louis's temperament, it is suggested that Lucas took great risks in losing the king's support if it was thought that his accounts were in any way exaggerated for public consumption or royal gullibility.

In summary, Lucas states that while traveling in Natolia, he came across a small mosque (in the city of Broussa, Turkey) with four dervishes inside. Lucas states that his guests received him with extreme hospitality and, in the custom of the day, invited him to share their meal with them. One of the dervishes was said to be from Uzebek (modern Uzbekistan) and was extremely well educated. Lucas says, "And I believe verily that he spoke all the languages in the world."

Their conversation began in Turkish but changed to Italian and then again to French. It was apparent that that dervish spoke at least Latin, Spanish, and Italian in addition to Turkish and French. Lucas states that his host's French was distinctly Parisian.

---

7 Ellie Crystal, "Nicholas Flamel," Crystalinks, http://www.crystalinks.com/flamel.html (accessed August 3, 2006).

Despite an outer appearance of about thirty years of age, the dervish confided to Lucas that he had retired to this location for study and meditation. He shared accounts of his own travels, giving the impression of being much older. In addition, he stated that he was one of seven wandering scholars who traveled the world seeking to perfect their studies and themselves. Upon parting, they promised to meet again in twenty years' time, and it was upon this meeting that Lucas had stumbled. Four of the seven friends were present, and the other three were expected to arrive soon. Many topics were covered in Lucas's conversation with the dervish, with philosophy, science, metaphysics, and esotericism dominating. The dervish explained to Lucas that a dervish was a philosopher, a person who has no bonds to the material world and yet has all power within his grasp because of his renunciation. He could live a thousand years if he so desired.

With this, the Philosopher's Stone was discussed and Flamel mentioned, the dervish informing Lucas that Flamel was indeed alive and that he had seen Nicholas and Perenelle only three years earlier in India. Lucas states that the dervish told him an unknown story of Abraham the Jew, the purported author of the book with which Flamel had discovered the keys to confecting the Philosopher's Stone. He said that three hundred years prior, an elderly member of their fraternity sought to visit his family in Paris once more before leaving for mystical retirement from the world. His friends sought to discourage him from making the journey, as it was long and dangerous. Upon reaching Paris, the elderly Jew found his family and even produced a demonstration of a transmutation to convince them that he had the secret. One family member sought to keep the elder sage from returning to his mystic brethren, and murdered him when he could not. For this, his punishment was to be burned alive. It was Flamel who later possessed the book written by the sage. In order to avoid a similar fate, or perhaps simply to escape from unwanted publicity, he arranged to fake his death, with Perenelle following suit.[8]

---

8 Patai, *The Jewish Alchemists*, 230.

THE TOMB

Flamel is said to have died at the age of 116 after a period of illness. However, other records state that he was 80. Perenelle went first, and Nicholas followed later that year. He left details on how he was to be buried in St. Jacques la Boucherie at the end of the nave. The tombstone was large, measuring 58 by 45 centimeters and 4 centimeters thick, and was designed to discourage grave robbers. In this task, it failed. Even the monthly masses arranged did not keep vandals away. His tomb was vandalized, and when it was opened by robbers, it was found empty.

St. Jaques la Boucherie was demolished in 1717. Flamel's headstone was later found in a grocer's shop in Rue des Arias, where its smooth marble back was used for chopping herbs and vegetables. Only when it was turned over was it discovered to be the headstone of the adept. The engravings on the stone were of a key with a sun above it and a closed book below it, and on the very top were engravings of Christ, St. Peter, and St. Paul—the symbols of his life.

HIS SUCCESSORS

With no children, the Flamel estate went to a nephew named Perrier, who had some interest in alchemy and presumably benefited from being such a close relative to the fourteenth century's greatest living alchemist. Giving access to Nicholas's papers and the prized book by Abraham the Jew, Flamel's bequest to Perrier was worth more than its weight in gold—if the process actually worked.

During the reign of Louis XIII, a descendent of Flamel, Dubois, seems to have taken to the bad habit of public demonstrations of transmutation—a practice made worse by the fact that it seems it was a supply of the powder that Dubois possessed, and not the knowledge to replenish it. When his store was used up, he found himself imprisoned in Vincennes. Richelieu had him condemned to death on account of past offenses and confiscated his property, with it the Book of Abraham the Jew, annotated in Flamel's own hand. Richelieu had a laboratory at Chateau du Rueil but seems to have had little success in deciphering the book's text or images. It was during this period that Nicholas's tomb was broken into and was said to have been found empty. The properties attached to the Flamels were ransacked at various times by those seeking the projection powder.

Apparently, copies of the book were made, or at least the images, and these would surface from time to time, with the copy in the Paris Bibliotheque Nationale (Ms Francais 14765) being the most complete.[9]

MODERN SCHOOLS OF FLAMEL

It is not surprising that several modern schools of alchemy and alchemical research undertake the "Path of Flamel" as an operative practice in their search for the Philosopher's Stone. One of the more peculiar aspects of the Flamel Path, or even mineral alchemy in general, is the tremendous amount of energy that it generates.

The following statements were made regarding the Flamel Path during a part of the operation known as "Flying Eagles," in which mercury is distilled to increasing levels of purity and, as such, power. The operation took place in the fall of 1993.

The author states:

> At that time, I had an experience which was both physical and "subtle" which convinced me that the distillation of amalgams can create a force field of significant proportions. Further, I was satisfied by certain facts of the experiment that there was no self-delusion nor expectation of an experience on my part, and that the force field induces chemical changes within the operator. "The secret of alchemy is this: there is a way of manipulating matter and energy so as to create a force-field. . . . The vital thing is not the transmutation of metals, but of the experimenter himself."[10]

---

9 Patai, *The Jewish Alchemists*, 226.

10 This quote is from *The Morning of the Magicians*, by Louis Pauwels and Jacques Bergier, a disputed work that makes an important and critical point regarding alchemy.

> . . . A friend of mine has had similar experiences in work on the vegetable kingdom. It is my hope that sharing the experience will encourage others to discuss the circumstances of change in themselves that have come from their work.[11]

FLAMEL: FACT IN FICTION

Although it seems that Nicholas Flamel's life and legendary pilgrimage is well documented, several clues throughout history and within his own accounts lead one to wonder if the factual account of Flamel's legend withstands the critics of those in the know of the "gay science."[12]

Indeed, the most famous alchemical author of all time, who is even cited in contemporary children's books and movies, has a very unusual name. *Nicholas* is derived from the Greek word meaning "conqueror of the stone," and *Flamel* is of course the juxtaposition of *flame* and *El*, giving us "the Conqueror Stone of the Holy Flame," or "Conqueror of the Holy Fire Stone."

The most famous copy of the manuscript of Abraham (or "a Brahmin") the Jew, presently kept in the Bibliotheque Nationale de Paris, was written by a Chevalier Denis Molinier. We are at first stunned by the word *Chevalier*, which was not a title of nobility in the seventeenth century, when he allegedly wrote this copy from a former manuscript or the original itself. In reality, *Chevalier* is literally translated as *knight* in English, meaning "a soldier on a horse." This is very similar to Qabalist (or Cabalist) in the ancient usages.

Here we must note that by tradition, because of the Holy Inquisition and also as a means to repel the unworthy, alchemists and Qabalists of the past were very familiar with puns and plays on words, as well as borrowing from dead languages. All the educated gentry of old Europe was busy creating such anagrams, using ciphers as simple intellectual challenges.

---

11 Russ House, "Force Fields, Fulcanelli and Flamel," special issue for Sacred Space, *The Stone*, no. 12 (1997): 22.

12 The "gay science" is an ancient name for alchemy.

We must look at the name of Chevalier Denis Molinier from this same state of mind, and the following work must be done in the original language. Here in French we have:

Chevalier Denis Moligner

Cavalier Sine(D) Minier

Cabale D(de) Miniere

In Greek B=V

La Cabale est la miniere de l'Or.

Translated in English: "Cabala is the source of Gold."

Also, *Molinier* can be separated into *Mol* (soft, puttylike) and *in-ier*, which sounds like *igné* (igneous). In the laboratory, these are the qualities of the Philosopher's Stone: a soft, fiery substance as well as a knowledge of all Western esoteric sciences. Indeed, in the old days, one was not so much an alchemist or a Qabalist as a person pursuing alchemy, Qabala, and astrology as a triptych of the unified art and science of Hermeticism.

What about another famous author, such as Basilius Valentine, which Latin translation gives as "Powerful King"? *King* can also be understood as Regulus, the first step in the preparation of the stibnite with iron, which gives the preparatory stage of the Stone its magnetic life. Does this mean that the ancients knew more than they said?[13]

---

13 Indeed. Place yourself back in 1940. All the countries in the world were looking for a way to split the atom. In France, Joliot-Curie, son-in-law of the famous Marie Curie, was working on heavy water and uranium. When the Germans stormed through France, one of their first targets was his laboratory, located on Rue Ampere in Ivry sur Seine, an eastern suburb of Paris. There they found nothing. The ten tons of heavy water had been shipped to the United States a few days before, and the uranium had been cast into tiles of the floor of the laboratory. At the time, the Germans, the Italians, and the French were all working on paths that led nowhere. Joliot-Curie was about to make his battery divergent, and he didn't know it. A good thing this never happened! What is most surprising is that when the United States embarked on the Manhattan Project in 1942 to make an atomic bomb, they went for the only two methods that worked in those days—using uranium and plutonium—and succeeded in less than three years. Some say that an alchemist had given the Americans the key to make it work.

But let's go back to our story, the legendary Flamel and his pilgrimage to St. Jacques de Compostella, to find the meaning of the book. In those days, many people undertook this journey. A modern equivalent would be the pilgrimage to Mecca that any good Muslim is supposed to undertake during his lifetime. Some went on foot; richer ones on horseback. Coming from all over Europe, one of their gathering points was Paris, where Nicholas allegedly started his journey. Little is known of this first leg of his trip by land, except that he reaches Montjoye (Mount of Joy), but much more is known of the return by sea. This is because the Dry Way (by land) is reputedly much faster than the Wet Way (by sea).

Once in Compostella (Field of the Star), Nicholas embarks on a ship, where he meets a merchant from Boulogne, a French seaport. We leave to your sagacity to decipher the Boulogne part, but we would like to point out that this man is a merchant. Why? Because the god Mercury was reputed to be the patron saint of merchants (as well as of thieves, but that's a whole different story). In confidence, the merchant introduces Flamel to a reputed wise man, Master Canches (the white, the Sulfur) who lives in Leon (anagram of *Noel*, or Christmas, a subtle hint at Tiphareth or the Sun, the Christ state of consciousness, which is the state an adept acquires once in possession of the Philosopher's Stone) and who travels with Nicholas back to Paris and, during the journey, deciphers for him the meaning behind the illustrations of the book. On the way to the city of Orleans (anagram of "L'or es an," or "Gold is in"), Master Canches starts vomiting profusely and dies seven days into his illness, terrified that Flamel would leave him. Indeed, the sulphur will give its soul to the mercury and after seven philosophical days is conjoined so intimately with the mercury that the whole becomes a perfect union.

The first time Nicholas Flamel does the projection is in the company of his soul mate, Perenelle (perennial), on Monday, January 17, 1382, when he transmutes half a pound of mercury into pure silver. As it turns out, a simple calculation shows that this specific date was a Friday. When we know that the days of the weeks are linked to different metals and planetary influences, we wonder what Flamel transmuted on that day. Furthermore, the second transmutation occurred on April 25 of the same year, which would have been a Friday once again. Since Friday is linked to Venus and copper, we have to take into consideration that it is mentioned that the cover of the Book of Abraham the Jew was made of finely delineated copper. Whoever heard of such a cover for a book?

As a student who has practiced for a long time at the furnace, we must add here that the book, available in English thanks to the translation made by one of our friends, is the most candid explanation of what is known as the Flamel Path, one of the ways to the Stone. Unfortunately, it still requires a good twenty years of one's life full-time, as well as a good deal of money, to reach the aim of this path—perhaps not very compatible with our modern lifestyle.

Pater Ace Zelim.[14]

Key Points

- Nicholas and Perenelle Flamel were real people who lived in the fourteenth century.

- Nicholas Flamel had a dream in which he would receive a book. The messenger took the form of an angel.

- Nicholas studied for twenty-one years before traveling to Spain to find a rabbi who could instruct him in Qabala so that he could decipher the manuscript.

- Upon receiving instruction, Flamel returned to Paris, where within three years he and Perenelle created the Philosopher's Stone and transmuted mercury in silver, and later into gold.

- Legends of the Flamels' survival abound in common and esoteric literature.

---

14 This symbolic interpretation of the journey of Flamel was given to us by an anonymous student of the Flamel Path.

- Many people have taken an interest in Flamel, as they seek the Philosopher's Stone for personal and selfish reasons.

- Modern practitioners of the Flamel Path state that mineral alchemy produces a force field that produces chemical and psychic changes in the operator.

GENERAL ASSIGNMENTS FOR APPENDIX C

1. Read about fourteenth-century France and Spain. Collect images of Paris, Leon, and other major cities. Allow them to sink into you and stimulate your imagination.

2. Begin reading a book on Qabala, such as Dion Fortune's *The Mystical Qabalah* or Gareth Knight's *A Practical Guide to Qabalistic Symbolism*. Have a special notebook for when you read, dividing it into sections for History, Theory and Philosophy, Practical Exercises, and any results of meditations you may have done, just as you have for your alchemical studies.

MEDITATION PRACTICES FOR APPENDIX C

1. Read the story of Nicholas Flamel. Imagining that you are Flamel, go through each step, starting with the angelic dream and ending with your own transition. Use the alternate ending as well, meeting the dervish in India and continuing to live until at least the eighteenth century. Carefully note your experiences and responses to this form of alchemical pathworking.

2. Meditate on what it would be like to undertake the Flamel Path or similar mineral work. Imagine yourself before a furnace, the heat intense, and feel the ensuing psychic force field that it creates. What is this like? How does it affect you?

3. Meditate on the nature of the furnace, its heat, and the idea of fire or energy in transmutation. What is this like? Where is the furnace in you? How has studying alchemy changed your life?

4. Repeat your earlier meditations on the Philosopher's Stone. What is it like? What does it impart? Spend much time on these meditations.

GLOSSARY

The exact meaning of specialized terms used in alchemy is always a tricky business. Many words are used in several different manners, such as *salt* and *mercury*, thereby adding to the confusion. The following definitions are given to assist aspiring alchemists in developing their own lexicons. When looking for the meaning of a specific alchemical term, always look to the source it is derived from and the context it is used in first, as this will help you to decipher the inner and outer meaning of the term. Difficult-to-pronounce words in Arabic, Greek, Hebrew, and Latin are followed by a pronunciation guide in italics.

Alchemy—(Arabic: *al-keh-mee*) The art and science of interior initiation and spiritual awakening that uses material operations to aid in the work as well as to demonstrate the actual efficiency of the process through the creation of plant and mineral products and tinctures. The most famous of these are the Philosopher's Stone and the Elixir of Life.

Angel Water—The liquefied potassium carbonate used in the creation of an Ens. Angel Water is created only during the spring months, when the ambient life force is increasing. Angel Water is caustic and should be handled carefully.

Calcination—(Latin: *kahl-sin-ay-shun*) Reducing plant residue to a fine ash after it has been used in the creation of a tincture.

Caput Mortuum—(Latin: *cah-poot mort-ehm*) Literally "dead head." See *Feces*.

Chaos—The primordial essence from which everything arises. See *Hyle*.

Circulation—Creating a tincture by percolating it. The herb is placed in a container that allows for the menstruum to evaporate and drip back onto the herb. A low heat is often used.

Correspondences—The relationship between energy, matter, and consciousness in the visible and invisible realms through analogy.

Distillation—Purifying a solid or liquid through heat and evaporation. Distillation allows the alchemist to remove minerals from water, thereby creating distilled water; to separate alcohol from red wine, thereby producing a menstruum for creating tinctures; and to separate the constituent parts of a tincture—sulphur and mercury—for the further refinement of the tincture. Distillation is the primary tool of the alchemist.

Elements—There are four basic elements or expressions of energy and matter in alchemy: fire, air, water, and earth. The manipulation of these elements is part of the alchemical process. The three essentials represent a specific relationship between them, and together, they represent two means of expressing the underlying harmony that alchemy seeks to express.

Elixir—A tincture that is refined, sometimes known as a Magisterium. It can also be a tincture composed of more than one plant. Elixirs use the parts of a plant that have medicinal value.

Ens—(Latin: *ehns*) A special tincture produced with Angel Water and generally made for initiatic purposes.

Feces—Residue after certain alchemical operations. This can refer to the plant matter prior to its calcination that remains after the creation of a tincture or to oils that are separated from distilled products.

Fermentation—Soaking a plant in fresh rain or distilled water at room temperature to create a tincture.

Greater Circulation—A phrase sometimes applied to working with minerals, as well as the spiritual or interior aspects of alchemy.

Great Work—The entire work from beginning to end; learning the secrets of transmutation in all three kingdoms for the purpose of self-perfection.

Hermes—A Greek god who was associated with the Egyptian god Thoth, thereby combining the two into Thoth-Hermes, and later simply assuming the duties of Thoth completely. Hermes is the patron deity of Hermeticism, of which alchemy is one of the chief operative arts and sciences.

Hyle—The primordial essence from which everything arises. See *Chaos*.

Kingdoms—The three main areas of life in alchemical practice. These are the plant, mineral, and animal kingdoms.

Leaching—A process in which plant salts are soaked in distilled water in order to draw out any water-soluble salts that were not separated during the creation of a tincture.

Lesser Circulation—A phrase sometimes applied to spagyrics in preparation for mineral work, or simply in reference to the physical methods of alchemy.

Maceration—Creating a tincture by placing the fresh or dried herb in alcohol.

Magisterium—(Latin: *mah-gist-ear-ee-uhm*) A tincture that has been highly refined through repeated maceration and distillation. Sometimes known as an Elixir.

Menstruum—A liquid used in the creation of a spagyric or alchemical product; usually pure alcohol or distilled water.

Mercury—One of the three essentials; the carrier of life force in a particular kingdom. In the plant kingdom, alcohol is the carrier of life energy; in the mineral kingdom, it is metallic mercury; and in the animal kingdom, it is blood.

Natural Magic—Occult operations that utilize energies of nature found in matter in connection with planetary cycles.

Niter—The energies of life and consciousness that come from Chaos or Hyle. Combined with salt, they give rise to the four elements and the three essentials.

Planetary Hours—A cyclic expression of the influences of the planetary energies across the week, as well as their variation each day. Charting of planetary hours starts on Saturday and follows the descent of the energies on the Tree of Life. Because of their regularity, planetary hours are used extensively in spagyrics, alchemy, and natural magic.

Plant Stone—An actual physical object created out of the separation and recombination of the salt, mercury, and sulphur of a plant. These

"Stones" are often small and hard like a pebble, but they may also be soft like licorice. A hard Stone is often used to create a homeopathic-like tincture in water and should not degrade over time despite constant immersion.

Quintessence—The pure and essential life energy in a plant, mineral, animal, or kingdom, brought to fruition and expression through alchemical practices. The elements in balance, or in perfect proportion to each other, is also known as the Quintessence.

Red Stone—The Philosopher's Stone, also known as the Stone of the Wise, the goal of alchemy. The Red Stone is a physical expression of an interior initiation in the alchemist's own consciousness. The Red Stone gives outer confirmation that such a state has been achieved and that the alchemist is not deluding him or herself. In Qabala, this would be a permanent initiation into Tiphareth, or the Sun. Also known as the Red Lion.

Salt—The basis of physical life; the material matrix of any physical object, be it plant, mineral, or animal. Salt contains powerful mineral energies that are refined and essential in the creation of spagyric and mineral products. Salt on the cosmic scale is the basis of all matter and, combined with niter, gives rise to the four elements and the three essentials, one of which bears its name.

Solve et Coagula—(Latin: *sol-vay eht koh-ag-ulah*) "Separate and recombine," the basis of all alchemical operations. Through the process of separation, energies of a person, plant, or mineral become more subtle and potent; through recombination, the physical body or form is able to absorb and utilize more energy.

Spagyrics—(Greek: *spah-jir-iks*) A subspecialty of alchemy that produces tinctures, Stones, and other products from plants. The term *spagyrics* was coined by Paracelsus and comes from the Greek equivalent of "solve et coagula." The procedures utilized in spagyrics are identical to those used in mineral alchemy, and therefore many students learn the basic procedures by working with plants before moving on to the more technically demanding mineral work.

Sulphur—The individualized essence of a plant, mineral, or animal; one of the three essentials. In plants, it is composed primarily of essential oils; in minerals, it is referred to as an oil; and in animals, it is consciousness, or the soul.

Thoth—The Egyptian god of wisdom, associated with the Greek god Hermes and the Roman god Mercury. Thoth was the supreme god of magic in ancient Egypt and the patron deity of alchemy.

Three Essentials—Everything is made of three parts, or essentials. These are its salt, mercury, and sulphur. The separating and recombining of the three essentials is the basis for all spagyric and alchemical procedures.

Tincture—The product resulting from the immersion of a fresh or dried plant into a menstruum to remove the sulphur from the salt. Tinctures are generally made with alcohol that is 90% to 95% pure and a single plant or herb. Tinctures can be made from resins, bark, roots, leafs, stems, or any other part of a plant or plant byproduct. Spagyric tinctures are unique in that, unlike herbal tinctures, the plant matter from which they are created is calcined and added to the product.

White Stone—A significant step in mineral alchemy is the creation of the White Stone. Identical to the Red Stone, only less powerful, the White Stone demonstrates mastery over the lunar or astral worlds.

For additional alchemical terms and their various meanings, see:

Greer, John Michael. *The New Encyclopedia of the Occult*. St. Paul, MN: Llewellyn Publications, 2003.

Johnson, Kenneth Rayner. *The Fulcanelli Phenomenon*. Jersey, Channel Islands, UK: Neville Spearman, Ltd., 1980. See: Glossary.

Jolande Jacobi, ed. *Paracelsus: Selected Writings*. Bollingen Series XXVIII. Princeton, NJ: Princeton University Press, 1951. See: Glossary.

Lapidus. *In Pursuit of Gold: Alchemy Today in Theory and Practice*. Jersey, Channel Islands, UK: Neville Spearman, Ltd., 1976. See: Glossary.

Pernety, Antoine-Joseph. *An Alchemical Treatise on the Great Art*. Foreword by Todd Pratum. York Beach, ME: Weiser, 1995. See: Addenda: Dictionary of Hermetic Symbols from Albert Poisson's *Theories et Symbols des Alchemistes*.

SELECTED BIBLIOGRAPHY

Albertus, Frater. *The Alchemist's Handbook*. York Beach, ME: Weiser, 1987.

———. *Praxis Spagyrica Philosophica: Plain and Honest Directions on How to Make the Stone; and, From "One" to "Ten": A Treatise on the Origin and Extension of the Prime Manifestation on the Physical Plane*. York Beach, ME: Weiser, 1998.

Carey, George Washington, and Inez Eudora Perry. *The Zodiac and the Salts of Salvation: Homeopathic Remedies for the Sign Types*. York Beach, ME: Weiser, 1996.

Caron, M., and S. Hutin. *The Alchemists*. Translated by Helen R. Lane. New York: Grove Press, Inc., 1961.

Cockren, Archibald. *Alchemy Rediscovered and Restored*. Whitefish, MT: Kessinger Publishing, n.d.

Danciger, Elizabeth. *Homeopathy: From Alchemy to Medicine*. Rochester, VT: Healing Arts Press, 1987.

de Rola, Stanislas Klossowski, *Alchemy: The Secret Art*. London: Thames and Hudson, 1973.

———. *The Golden Game: Alchemical Engravings of the Seventeenth Century*. New York: Thames and Hudson, 1997.

Dubuis, Jean. *Fundamentals of Esoteric Knowledge*. Lessons 1–12. Winfield, IL: Triad Publishing, n.d. (Sample lessons available online at http://www.triad-publishing.com/Course_eso.html.)

————. *Mineral Alchemy*. 4 vols: Lessons 1–84. Winfield, IL: Triad Publishing, n.d. (Sample lesson available online at http://www.triad-publishing.com/Course_alc.html.)

————. *Spagyrics: A Course in Plant Alchemy*. 2 vols: Lessons 1–24 and Lessons 25–48. Winfield, IL: Triad Publishing, n.d. (Sample lesson available online at http://www.triad-publishing.com/Course_spg.html.)

Fortune, Dion, and Gareth Knight. *The Circuit of Force*. Loughbrough, UK: Thoth Publications, 1998.

————. *The Mystical Qabalah*. York Beach, ME: Weiser, 2000.

Gerber, Richard. *Vibrational Medicine*. Santa Fe, NM: Bear and Co., 1996.

Gilchrist, Cherry. *The Elements of Alchemy*. Rockport, MA: Element Books, 1991.

Godwin, Joscelyn, trans. and ed. *Salomon Trismosin's Splendor Solis*. Grand Rapids, MI: Phanes Press, 1991.

Junius, Manfred. *The Practical Handbook of Plant Alchemy*. Rochester, VT: Healing Arts Press, 1985.

McLean, Adam. *The Alchemical Mandala: A Survey of the Mandala in the Western Esoteric Traditions*. 2nd ed. Grand Rapids, MI: Phanes Press, 2002.

Reid, John III. *John Reid's Course on Practical Alchemy*. The Alchemy Web Site. http://www.levity.com/alchemy/johnreid.html (accessed July 7, 2006).

ALCHEMICAL READING
LIST AND RESOURCES

Over the last decade, there has been an explosion in the amount of resources available to the aspiring alchemist. There is so much available that at times it can be difficult to decide where to begin. However, alchemy has always been fraught with hucksters and con men. Courses offering degrees, certificates, and other forms of validation are fine for professional continuing education, but in alchemy they mean little or nothing. In the end, one has either completed the inner and outer work or one hasn't, and a piece of paper will only show that someone has shown up for class and paid a fee. Be careful of promises of the fantastic.

The good news is that the worldwide alchemical circle is a small one, and it is easy to contact many people courtesy of the Internet. In fact, for the would-be alchemist, the Internet is the best place to start. Adam McLean's Alchemy Web Site (www.levity.com/alchemy) is world famous and has thousands of documents, images, and articles on alchemy. There are free course materials listed as well as links to other sites, e-groups, and various chats.

For those looking for a quality self-paced study course that covers all of the possible permutations of plant and mineral work, there is the course work previously issued by the Philosophers of Nature, now available through Triad Publishing. With forty-eight lessons on spagyrics and eighty-four lessons on mineral work, these courses have been the guiding hand for thousands of sincere students across the world and are available at an affordable price.

Several individuals who have studied with Frater Albertus and Manfred Junius continue to teach what they have learned and can be found in Australia, the United States, and Europe. Such instruction is invaluable when it can be had, in that it connects each student to the living tradition and saves hours of having to learn by trial and error. Both books by these modern alchemical giants should be in every library.

The following books have been selected because of their importance, availability, and practicality to new and even advanced students of the Hermetic arts and sciences. Combined, they create a complete course in alchemical theory and practice for the disciplined and dedicated student and will give a complete foundation for intermediate and advanced alchemical, esoteric, or energetic healing practices.

SUGGESTED READING

Practical Alchemy

An Alchemical Treatise on the Great Art, by Antoine-Joseph Pernety

The Alchemical Works of Geber, translated by Richard Russell

The Alchemist's Handbook, by Frater Albertus

Culpeper's Medicine: A Practice of Western Holistic Medicine, by Graeme Tobyn

The Hermetic and Alchemical Writings of Paracelsus the Great, by A. E. Waite

In Pursuit of Gold: Alchemy Today in Theory and Practice, by Lapidus

John Reid's Course on Practical Alchemy, by John Reid, III, an e-book located at http://www.levity.com/alchemy/johnreid.html

The Practical Handbook of Plant Alchemy, by Manfred Junius

Praxis Spagyrica Philosophica: Plain and Honest Directions on How to Make the Stone; and, From "One" to "Ten": A Treatise on the Origin and Extension of the Prime Manifestation on the Physical Plane, by Frater Albertus (This is actually two books issued as one.)

Homeopathy and Alchemy

Homeopathy: From Alchemy to Medicine, by Elizabeth Danciger

The Zodiac and the Salts of Salvation: Homeopathic Remedies for the Sign Types, by George Washington Carey and Inez Eudora Perry

Alchemical Meditations and Inner Alchemy

The Alchemical Mandala: A Survey of the Mandala in the Western Esoteric Traditions, by Adam McLean

Alchemical Studies, by C. G. Jung, translated by R. F. C. Hull

Psychic Energy: Its Source and Its Transformation, by M. Esther Harding, with foreword by C. G. Jung

Salomon Trismosin's Splendor Solis, translated and edited by Joscelyn Godwin, with introduction and commentary by Adam McLean

General Esoteric Theory and Practice

The Art & Practice of Creative Visualization, by Ophiel

The Hermetic Tradition: Symbols and Teachings of the Royal Art, by Julius Evola

The Isaiah Effect: Decoding the Lost Science of Prayer and Prophecy, by Gregg Braden

The Kybalion, by Three Initiates

Psychosynthesis: A Collection of Basic Writings, by Roberto Assagioli, M.D.

The Seven Rays of the QBL, by Frater Albertus

Alchemical Images and Plates

Alchemy: The Secret Art, by Stanislas Klossowski de Rola

Alchemy & Mysticism, by Alexander Roob

The Golden Game: Alchemical Engravings of the Seventeenth Century, by Stanislas Klossowski de Rola

History

Access to Western Esotericism, by Antoine Faivre

The Alchemists, by M. Caron and S. Hutin, translated by Helen R. Lane

Alchemy Rediscovered and Restored, by Archibald Cockren

The Elements of Alchemy, by Cherry Gilchrist

Hidden Wisdom: A Guide to the Western Inner Traditions, by Richard Smoley and Jay Kinney

Lure and Romance of Alchemy, by C. J. S. Thompson

Modern Esoteric Spirituality, edited by Antoine Faivre and Jacob Needleman

Fulcanelli and Alchemical Mysteries

The Dwellings of the Philosophers, by Fulcanelli, translated by Brigitte Donvez and Lionel Perrin

The Fulcanelli Phenomenon, by Kenneth Rayner Johnson

Fulcanelli: Master Alchemist; The Mystery of the Cathedrals, translated by Mary Sworder

The Mysteries of the Great Cross of Hendaye: Alchemy and the End of Time, by Jay Weidner and Vincent Bridges

Quantum Physics and Energetic Healing

The Dancing Wu Li Masters: An Overview of the New Physics, by Gary Zukav

The Dreaming Universe: A Mind-Expanding Journey into the Realm Where Psyche and Physics Meet, by Fred Alan Wolf, Ph.D.

Fire in the Mind: Science, Faith, and the Search for Order, by George Johnson

The Holographic Universe, by Michael Talbot

Vibrational Medicine, by Richard Gerber, M.D.

What the Bleep Do We Know!?, DVD, directed by William Arntz, Betsy Chasse, and Mark Vicente (The movie's website is a small treasure trove of articles on quantum physics and includes links to the Institute of Noetic Science, a forerunner in new and cutting-edge research on the mind-matter interface: www.whatthebleep.com.)

SPAGYRIC AND ALCHEMICAL COURSES

Spagyrics: A Course in Plant Alchemy, by Jean Dubuis, Lessons 1–48
Mineral Alchemy, by Jean Dubuis, Lessons 1–84
Triad Publishing, P.O. Box 116, Winfield, IL 60190
Tel: 630.682.3938; Fax: 630.665.2364
Email: info@triad-publishing.com
Website: http://www.triad-publishing.com

Triad also hosts occasional seminars and workshops on various aspects of Western esotericism.

INTERNET

The Alchemy Web Site—www.levity.com/alchemy
Adam McLean is the owner of this international treasure. It is one-stop shopping that will allow you to connect with safe and reliable alchemical resources.

SEMINARS AND WORKSHOPS

Institute for Hermetic Studies
P.O. Box 4513, Wyoming, PA 18644-4513
Website: www.hermeticinstitute.org

The Institute for Hermetic Studies offers seminars and workshops on all aspects of Western esotericism, including plant and mineral alchemy. For a subscription to *VOXHERMES*, the Institute's free electronic newsletter announcing both Institute and non-Institute seminars and activities, contact info@hermeticinstitute.org.

INDEX

GET MORE AT LLEWELLYN.COM

Visit us online to browse hundreds of our books and decks, plus sign up to receive our e-newsletters and exclusive online offers.

- Free tarot readings • Spell-a-Day • Moon phases
- Recipes, spells, and tips • Blogs • Encyclopedia
- Author interviews, articles, and upcoming events

GET SOCIAL WITH LLEWELLYN

Find us on
Facebook

www.Facebook.com/LlewellynBooks

Follow us on

www.Twitter.com/Llewellynbooks

GET BOOKS AT LLEWELLYN

LLEWELLYN ORDERING INFORMATION

Order online: Visit our website at www.llewellyn.com to select your books and place an order on our secure server.

Order by phone:
- Call toll free within the U.S. at 1-877-NEW-WRLD (1-877-639-9753)
- Call toll free within Canada at 1-866-NEW-WRLD (1-866-639-9753)
- We accept VISA, MasterCard, and American Express

Order by mail:
Send the full price of your order (MN residents add 6.875% sales tax) in U.S. funds, plus postage and handling to: Llewellyn Worldwide, 2143 Wooddale Drive Woodbury, MN 55125-2989

POSTAGE AND HANDLING:
STANDARD (U.S. & Canada):
(Please allow 12 business days)
$25.00 and under, add $4.00.
$25.01 and over, FREE SHIPPING.

INTERNATIONAL ORDERS (airmail only):
$16.00 for one book, plus $3.00 for each additional book.

Visit us online for more shipping options. Prices subject to change.

FREE CATALOG!

To order, call
1-877-
NEW-WRLD
ext. 8236
or visit our
website

Encyclopedia
of Natural Magic
JOHN MICHAEL GREER

Natural magic is the ancient and powerful art of using material substances—herbs, stones, incenses, oils, and much more—to tap into the hidden magical powers of nature, transforming your surroundings and yourself.

Not just a cookbook of spells, the *Encyclopedia of Natural Magic* provides an introduction to the philosophy underlying this system. It also gives detailed information on 176 different herbs, trees, stones, metals, oils, incenses, and other substances, and offers countless ways to put them to magical use. With this book and a visit to your local herb store, rock shop, or backyard garden, you're ready to enter the world of natural magic!

0-7387-0674-4
312 pp., 7½ x 9⅛, illus.   **$18.95**

Cunningham's
Encyclopedia of Magical Herbs
SCOTT CUNNINGHAM

This is the most comprehensive source of herbal data for magical uses ever printed! Almost every one of the over four hundred herbs are illustrated, making this a great source for herb identification. For each herb you will also find: magical properties, planetary rulerships, genders, associated deities, folk and Latin names, and much more. To make this book even easier to use, it contains a folk name cross-reference, and all of the herbs are fully indexed. There is also a large annotated bibliography, and a list of mail-order suppliers so you can find the books and herbs you need. Like all of Cunningham's books, this one does not require you to use complicated rituals or expensive magical paraphernalia. Instead, it shares with you the intrinsic powers of the herbs. Thus, you will be able to discover which herbs, by their very nature, can be used for luck, love, success, money, divination, astral projection, safety, psychic self-defense, and much more. This book has rapidly become the classic in its field and is a must for all Wiccans.

0-87542-122-9
336 pp., 6 x 9, illus.   **$16.95**

A Garden of Pomegranates
Skrying on the Tree of Life

ISRAEL REGARDIE, EDITED AND ANNO-
TATED BY CHIC AND SANDRA TABATHA CICERO

Long considered the best single introduction to the Qabalah for magicians, the third edition of Israel Regardie's *A Garden of Pomegranates* is
now better than ever, thanks to the extensive annotations and new material by Chic Cicero and Sandra Tabatha Cicero. Their work has made A
Garden of Pomegranates easier to understand, more complete, and up
to date. It now includes over 300 pages of never-before-published information from two Senior Adepts of the Hermetic Order of the Golden
Dawn.

978-1-56718-141-8
552 pp., 6 x 9, illus. $21.95

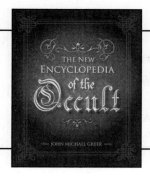

The New Encyclopedia of the Occult
JOHN MICHAEL GREER

From "Aarab Zereq" to "Zos Kia Cultus," it's the most complete occult reference work on the market. With this one text, you will gain a thorough overview of the history and current state of the occult from a variety of North American and western European traditions. Its pages offer the essential knowledge you need to make sense of the occult, along with references for further reading if you want to learn more.

You will find the whole range of occult tradition, lore, history, philosophy, and practice in the Western world. *The New Encyclopedia of the Occult* includes magic, alchemy, astrology, divination, Tarot, palmistry, geomancy, magical orders such as the Golden Dawn and Rosicrucians, Wiccan, Thelema, Theosophy, modern Paganism, and biographies of important occultists.

1-56718-336-0
608 pp., 8 x 10   **$34.99**

Magical Herbalism
The Secret Craft of the Wise

Scott Cunningham

Certain plants are prized for the special range of energies—the vibrations, or powers—they possess. *Magical Herbalism* unites the powers of plants and man to produce, and direct, change in accord with human will and desire.

This is Magic that is beautiful and natural—a craft of hand and mind merged with the power and glory of nature: a special kind that does not use the medicinal powers of herbs, but rather the subtle vibrations and scents that touch the psychic centers and stir the astral field in which we live to work at the causal level behind the material world.

This is the Magic of Enchantment . . . of word and gesture to shape the images of mind and channel the energies of the herbs. It is a Magic for everyone—for the herbs are easily and readily obtained, the tools are familiar or easily made, and the technology that of home and garden. This book includes step-by-step guidance to the preparation of herbs and to their compounding in incense and oils, sachets and amulets, simples and infusions, with simple rituals and spells for every purpose.

0-87542-120-2
288 pp., 5³⁄₁₆ x 8, illus.   **$13.99**

Homeopathy
An A to Z Home Handbook

ALAN V. SCHMUKLER

Effective, safe, affordable, and free of chemical side effects—the benefits of homeopathy are endless! Already established in the national health care systems of England, France, Germany, and the Netherlands, homeopathic treatments are used by over 500 million people worldwide. Alan Schmukler's *Homeopathy* discusses the history and science of this alternative medicine and provides a comprehensive list of proven remedies—safe for people *and* animals.

Packed with homeopathic treatments for arthritis, colds, food poisoning, insomnia, Lyme disease, morning sickness, wounds, and a host of other ailments and injuries, this handy reference guide also includes information on homeopathic immunization and first aid. Schmukler gives helpful instructions for matching remedies with symptoms, ingesting them correctly, making remedies at home, and stretching your supply.

0-7387-0873-9
408 pp., 6 x 9   **$17.95**

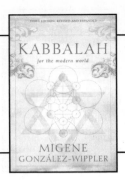

Kabbalah for the Modern World
MIGENE GONZÁLEZ-WIPPLER

A classic by the author of *Keys to the Kingdom*, this book was the first to present traditional Kabbalah from a scientific orientation—showing how it clearly relates to Quantum Theory, Relativity and the Big Bang. This guide to Kabbalah also explores Kabbalist principles, in addition to important rites, ritual, and magic. Also included are tables of the Hebrew alphabet, Divine names, planetary hours, correspondences related to the Tree of Life, and more!

0-7387-0987-5
288 pp., 5¼ x 8   **$13.95**

The Tree of Life
An Illustrated Study in Magic

ISRAEL REGARDIE, EDITED AND ANNOTATED
BY CHIC AND SANDRA TABATHA CICERO

In 1932, when magic was a "forbidden subject," Israel Regardie wrote *The Tree of Life* at the age of 24. He believed that magic was a precise scientific discipline as well as a highly spiritual way of life, and he took on the enormous task of making it accessible to a wide audience of eager spiritual seekers. The result was this book, which adroitly presents a massive amount of diverse material in a remarkably unified whole.

From the day it was first published, *The Tree of Life* has remained in high demand by ceremonial magicians for its skillful combination of ancient wisdom and modern magical experience. It was Regardie's primary desire to point out the principles of magic that cut across all boundaries of time, religion, and culture—those fundamental principles common to all magic, regardless of any specific tradition or spiritual path.

1-56718-132-5
552 pp., 6 x 9, illus., includes full-color, 4-pp. insert   **$24.95**

To Write to the Author

If you wish to contact the author or would like more information about this book, please write to the author in care of Llewellyn Worldwide and we will forward your request. Both the author and publisher appreciate hearing from you and learning of your enjoyment of this book and how it has helped you. Llewellyn Worldwide cannot guarantee that every letter written to the author can be answered, but all will be forwarded. Please write to:

Mark Stavish
⅋ Llewellyn Worldwide
2143 Wooddale Drive
Woodbury, MN 55125-2989

Please enclose a self-addressed stamped envelope for reply,
or $1.00 to cover costs. If outside U.S.A., enclose
international postal reply coupon.

Many of Llewellyn's authors have websites with additional information and resources. For more information, please visit our website at:
www.llewellyn.com